MEALS
in **30** MINUTES

🕐

Cheryl Townsley

Lifestyle for Health Publishing
P.O. Box 3871, Littleton, CO 80161

Graphics: Nick Zellinger
Text Design: Theresa Frank

This publication is designed to provide accurate and
authoritative information in regard to the subject matter
covered. It is sold with the understanding that the author
and the publisher are not engaged in rendering legal,
medical, or other professional service. If medical services
or other expert consultation is required, the services of a
competent professional should be sought.

Townsley, Cheryl
        Meals in 30 minutes /
    Cheryl Townsley
        Includes bibliographical references
        ISBN 0–9644566–0–5
        1. Cookbook. 2. Nutrition. 3. Health. I. Title.

For information contact:

Lifestyle for Health Publishing
P.O. Box 3871
Littleton, CO 80161
For ordering information, refer to the last page.

Printed in the United States of America

Contents

Part I:
Recipe Collection

Part II:
Creative Cooking

Part III:
Resources

Lord, thank you for a dear family ~
they love me through the tough times,
they encourage me to be my best,
but most of all, Thank You
for restoring my life
to live for You.

Acknowledgments

Many people have made this project possible. I especially want to thank my husband, Forest, and our daughter, Anna. They have patiently let me place "new recipes" on our plates for years. Thank you to a great family!

Thank you, Dr. Peter Petropulos, for your diagnosis and treatment of my total "crash" and subsequent turn to health.

Thank you, Theresa Frank, for your text design and editing abilities. Your ongoing support has been critical to my writing.

Thank you, Lory Floyd, for superb editing and attention to detail. Your eagle–sharp eyes leave no mistake unturned.

Thank you, Nick Zellinger, for an invigorating and fresh cover design.

Thank you, Lord, for the vision to "Feed My people." For with Your vision, comes Your provision. Without Your vision, Your people perish.

Introduction

It is unfortunate to me to see so many American families come home, gobble down "stuff" mistakenly taken as food in front of a TV, only to run on to other fast–paced activities. It is time to realize that a full and enriched life does not operate under those conditions. Life is more than an undisciplined appetite, whether for instant food, instant highs, more clothes, more wealth, etc.

Many people come into our home to relax and enjoy a wonderful meal. The meal begins when they walk in the door to a peaceful, orderly environment. What a haven that represents in this harried world. They sit down to an attractive table set with placemats, napkins and candles. A mouth–watering aroma tantalizes their taste buds. Then they are served a meal that they thoroughly enjoy. The food looks appealing and is colorful. When they place the food in their mouths, they experience the taste of "real" food prepared with love and attention.

What is your response right at this moment to that picture? Is it your family's lifestyle? It can be. On any budget, with any member working outside of the home. It simply takes some planning and the right tools.

We eat many of our meals in a peaceful home at an attractive table (set by Anna), with candles. We eat delicious food, and we take time to talk with each other about our individual days.

Do I spend all day in the kitchen? Do I spend all day cleaning? No, to each question. We have developed a lifestyle that reflects our priorities, and it is giving us more rewards than we can count or measure. We have a vision for our family, a plan to enact that vision and a commitment to work the plan.

It is from that experience that I give you these ideas. They are a beginning. However, to fully appreciate these meals, take a little time to set your table. Enjoy some music. Sit down at the table with a friend, or with your family, and spend some time . . . talking and listening to each other and enjoying your meal.

If this concept is foreign to you, start the practice once a week. Realize that this is a process. Don't be frustrated that you are not in the place that I described. It is a process that begins right where you are and lasts a lifetime. Don't rush the process and expect it to happen by tomorrow. You can't "instantize" or "microwave" a lifestyle. That takes time.

As I give you ideas to minimize the time spent preparing a meal, take just five minutes to create the "home" to enjoy the meal. Take five minutes longer to savor the meal and to spend time with your family. Ten minutes of our 24–hour day is a small investment to begin to bring a lifestyle of peace and health into your life. Don't you agree?

So, how can you use this book? I have found several principles to be quite important in our diet to achieve and maintain good health. I have worked off of these principles. (For more detail on each principle, please see my book, *Food Smart!,* published by Piñon Press, 1994.)

Food Combining and Food Timing

Knowing when to eat is as important as setting aside enough time to eat. The body operates on a schedule, whether we are aware of it or not. That clock leads the body into performing certain activities. That body cycle is shown below.

4:00 a.m. to 12:00 p.m. is elimination time. During this time body waste and food debris are eliminated. It is best to eat only fruits during this time. Fruits quickly digest and therefore minimally affect the elimination process.

12:00 p.m. to 8:00 p.m. is appropriation time. Eating and digestion occur during this time. Fruits, veggies, proteins and starches, in proper combinations, are eaten during this time.

8:00 p.m. to 4:00 a.m. is assimilation time. Food is absorbed and used during this part of the cycle. Food should not be eaten at this point.

All of us have eaten a late–night meal. The next morning we feel extremely fatigued. The reason is because during the night–time cycle (8:00 p.m. to 4:00 a.m.), the body is supposed to be absorbing nutrients and repairing the system from daily wear and tear.

Eating during this time robs the body of the energy necessary to absorb and digest nutrients. Digestion is a very energy–intensive mechanism. The body has little time for healing and rest while it's digesting. When the body has to digest food during this digestion–absorption cycle, the person will feel tired.

Since digestion requires so much energy, we need it to occur as efficiently and effectively as possible. This is where proper food combining is helpful. If foods are poorly combined, digestion can take up to eight hours to complete.

Properly combined food requires as little as three hours. Proper food combinations provide us with more energy, mental clarity, emotional stability and an ability to handle stress better.

Improper food combining results in energy loss, enzyme depletion and toxicity. Food putrefies in the digestive system, which leads to gas, bloating and poor elimination. All these results lead to sickness, excess weight and disease.

Food combining can be as intricate or as simple as you make it. I have simplified food combining into a couple of guidelines. Remember, these are guidelines, not laws. Work toward consistency, and ignore the temptation to become frustrated and quit.

> 1. Eat fruit 20 to 30 minutes before a meal or two to three hours after a meal. Melons should be eaten by themselves.

> 2. Never combine a protein and starch or two different proteins. Protein can be eaten with non–starchy vegetables. Starch can be eaten with vegetables.

Examples of protein are beans, nuts, seeds and meat. Starches are potatoes, grains, pasta and winter squash. Beans are an exception. Although a protein, they can be combined with starches (for example, beans and rice). Beans also include all soy products (tofu, tempeh, etc.).

If you're not a vegetarian, eat meat with salads or non–starchy vegetables. Otherwise, eat a baked potato with veggies instead of meat. Eat veggie sandwiches instead of meat and bread sandwiches. Use meat–free sauces on pasta.

These combinations may take some time to implement. Being aware of them is the first step. I found that good food combining also helped in my weight loss and weight stability. I did not have to sacrifice certain foods. Instead, I learned when and in what combinations to eat these foods.

These guidelines will get you started along the path of maximum digestion and utilization of food ingested in the body. They are noted in this book, to use if that option is of interest to you.

Wheat and Dairy Options
Wheat and dairy are two of the most common food allergies in this country. After removing wheat and dairy from our diet, Forest eliminated his asthma inhalers (which he had used for over 30 years). His asthma symptoms left. As a family we have virtually eliminated all congestion, colds, flu and other respiratory symptoms. Wheat–free and dairy–free options are shown throughout the book and in the substitutions. (Please see our *Lifestyle for Health* cookbook for more information on these substitutions.)

Refined Sugar
Refined sugar is a real killer in the American diet. It is interesting to note that Americans consume about 200 pounds of fruit per year. Yet, we consume sugar at an average rate of 125 pounds per year. That means that for every eight bites of fruit, a person eats five bites of plain sugar. That statistic is amazing.

Refined sugar has *no* nutritional value. Worse, it can cause chemical addictions more difficult to break than many drug habits. Refined sugar can cause cravings, emotional disorders, mental confusion, depression (even to the point of suicide), PMS and many other problems. I know this is possible, for I experienced each one of these problems. These symptoms have not operated in my body since I eliminated refined sugar from my diet.

The key to eliminating refined sugar is to learn which healthier options your body can tolerate. Many alternatives exist, some of which even diabetics have success using. I do not recommend using aspartame (Nutrasweet) as a safe substitute. Over 50% of the complaints to the FDA are aspartame related. Check out the natural substitutions in Appendix B of this book (for more detailed information, check out *Food Smart!* and our *Lifestyle for Health* cookbook).

Fats and Oils
It has become public knowledge that a low fat diet is important. However, did you know that many commonly accepted oils on the market today are actually rancid, chemically processed and totally unfit for human consumption and assimilation?

It is important to get the right kinds of oils into the body to accomplish many necessary body functions. Those functions include: weight control, reduced blood clotting, hormone balancing, water retention, high energy levels, proper blood pressure, strong immune system and healthy skin and hair.

(For more information, request a May/June issue of our *Lifestyle for Health Newsletter* for $2.00. See address on the order form.)

We use only expeller pressed oil (the label will state if it is expeller or cold processed). I personally recommend the use of the Spectrum brand of oils. They are superb in flavor and quality. We have also eliminated all hydrogenated oil from our diet. This includes shortenings, margarines and products using hydrogenated and/or partially hydrogenated oils. Be sure to check ingredient lists for these ingredients. Hydrogenated fats have had one or two molecules of hydrogen added. This makes the fat a substance foreign to the body, unable to be assimilated.

Caffeine

Caffeine is another stimulant that does not promote good health. If you choose to drink coffee, a couple of practices can be helpful. When possible use organic coffee (i.e., Frontier). Organic coffee is grown without DDT, which is used in third world countries where most coffee is grown. DDT has been outlawed in the U.S. due to its known impact on birth defects. It is estimated that organic coffee has half the caffeine of regular coffee. Also, when possible, use decaffeinated (using a CO_2 process) coffee.

Chocolate also has caffeine. In any of my recipes, you can reduce the cocoa by half and use half carob, or eliminate all of the cocoa and use all carob. The choice is yours.

In addition to these principles, you will find *Meals in 30 Minutes* loaded with many tips for quick meal preparation, and bulk cooking tips. Take advantage of these tips, and make your meals as simple a job as possible.

Breakfast

Based on the food combining and food timing principles briefly discussed in the Introduction, we have developed a fruit–only–for–breakfast approach for our family. Over the last several years, we have found this approach has worked well for us for increased energy, weight maintenance and overall ease of preparation.

We call our breakfast drink a "fruit smoothie." I have provided several options along with a variety of ingredients for fruit smoothies in the Breakfast Recipe chapter. Vary the ingredients by season, availability and taste. The options are endless. For the best food combining, the all–fruit recipes are best.

For each serving of our fruit smoothie, we add the following ingredients:

> 1 tsp. Kyo Green (see Appendix A)
> 1 tsp. Aged Kyolic Garlic (see Appendix A)
> 1 to 2 tsp. flaxseed oil (see Appendix A)
> 1 to 3 tsp. sesame seeds (rich in calcium)

Each of these ingredients are discussed in full in our *Lifestyle for Health* cookbook. Mid–morning we might add a whole grain muffin, pancake waffle or cereal. Recipes for those dishes can be found in the Side Dishes chapter.

Lunches and Dinners

In my *Lifestyle for Health* cookbook, I have a full chapter on meal planning. That chapter addresses the why's, how–to's and management techniques.

In *Meals in 30 Minutes*, I am providing specific breakfast, lunch and dinner recipes and menu options. With each recipe I provide you with several options and variations. This allow you, the "chef," to know a few basic recipes and yet with a few variations appear to be the master of many dishes.

In addition to the listed options and variations, I have provided two menu ideas. The "quick menu idea" includes additions to the basic lunch/dinner recipe to put a meal on the table as quickly as possible.

The "company menu idea" includes additions to the basic lunch/dinner recipe that provides more variety and interest. This option does require more time or more advanced planning. Try the various menus. Revise them and then begin to created your own. As you discover menus that work especially well for you with each recipe, record it in the "Your Favorite Menu" space. This can save you time in the future.

Recipes that freeze well are noted with a snowman graphic. Any special freezing instructions are noted at that time. Recipes that do not freeze well have no snowman graphic.

Creative Cooking

The creative cooking section is designed to help you develop culinary versatility. Replacing cooking marathons with cooking sprints will save you time, energy and money while still being enjoyable. This is a new section in our revised *Meals in 30 Minutes* and will be a big help to your overall meal management skills.

Resource Information

Appendix A: Supplementation
Appendix A presents basic supplementation suggestions for people who eat on the run. Knowing what supplements to use for various deficiencies can help you augment a diet that may not be as healthy as you would like. Many people desire to eat better, but it does take time to make the transition. Appendix A shares our success with both

cleansing (removing toxins) and building (taking the appropriate supplements for any given season).

Appendix B: Equivalents and Substitutions
Appendix B will help you know what to use in place of white sugar, white flour, hydrogenated fats and other less healthy ingredients. It will also help you know that one cup is equal to 16 tablespoons. This handy reference guide will be invaluable for many kitchen tasks.

Appendix C: Preferred Brands
Nothing is more frustrating than to be excited to eat healthy and try a health food brand that tastes awful! Unfortunately there are a few lemons in the orchard. Appendix C shares the brands our family has found to be tasty, affordable and also produces consistent results when used in recipes. We are not reimbursed for these preferred brand endorsements. We simply believe they are excellent products. *Food Smart!* also gives you how to find retailers for your individual area by contacting your nearest wholesaler.

Hopefully, you will find the newly revised *Meals in 30 Minutes* a real help in your daily mission to provide healthy and tasty food on a time and money budget. May you learn from our experiences and shorten your learning cycle. Healthy food . . . it is now within your grasp. Reach out and take it. Enjoy the food, and most of all, enjoy the benefits of being a whole, healthy person!

PART I:

Recipe Collection

BREAKFASTS

Fruit Smoothies:

Banana Pineapple Smoothie
Banana Strawberry Smoothie
Banana Orange Smoothie
Banana Date Smoothie
Banana Peach Smoothie
Melon Smoothie

Fruit Shakes

Almond Milk:

Strawberry Milk
Banana Milk
Apple Milk
Strawberry & Banana Shake
Peach Shake
Banana Shake
Carob Chip Shake

Fruit Smoothie

This is our basic breakfast beverage. It is more filling than plain fruit juice. Try the many options and then begin to create your own.

   1 cup strawberries, fresh — or frozen
   2 cups apple juice, unsweetened, unfiltered

Directions:

Blend in blender until smooth.

Notes:

Variations:

2 bananas, 1 cup strawberries, 2 cups fresh pineapple juice

2 bananas, 1 cup strawberries, 2 cups fresh juice, 2 tbsp. sunflower seeds, 2 tbsp. sesame seeds

2 bananas, 1 cup strawberries, 2 cups fresh orange juice

2 bananas, 1 large apple, 2 cups fresh apple juice, 2 pitted dates, 2 tbsp. sunflower seeds

2 bananas, 2 ripe peaches, 2 cups fresh juice — apple or orange

2 cups cantaloupe pieces, 2 cups fresh watermelon juice

Ingredient Substitutions:

Fresh or frozen bananas — or berries — can be used.

Use various in-season fruit to help with variety, price and flavor.

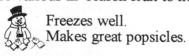 Freezes well.
Makes great popsicles.

Makes 3 cups
Serves 2

Nutritional Analysis:

Calories: 143 • Protein: (g) 1 • Carbs: (g) 34 • Fat: (g) 1 •
Sat. Fat: (g) 0 • Cholesterol: (mg) 0 • Fiber: (g) 2 • Sodium: (mg) 26

22

Fruit Shakes

A simple, yet tasty drink. Experiment with all different kinds of fruits. The tofu does not make perfect food combining.

1 block tofu, low–fat — 1 pkg. Mori Nu "lite" tofu, firm
3/4 cup soy milk — or rice or almond milk
2 whole bananas, frozen
1 cup strawberries, fresh —or frozen

Directions:

Blend all ingredients until blended smooth.

Notes:

Ingredient Substitution:

Soy or rice based "ice creams" can replace the tofu.

 Freezes well.

Makes 3–4 cups
Serves 2–3

Nutritional Analysis:

Calories: 225 • Protein: (g) 16 • Carbs: (g) 28 • Fat: (g) 7 •
Sat. Fat: (g) 0 • Cholesterol: (mg) 0 • Fiber: (g) 6 • Sodium: (mg) 16

Almond Milk

Almond milk is tasty by itself and a great substitute for dairy. It is easy to make in the blender. Almonds are high in calcium and easier to digest.

    1/2 cup almonds raw, shelled
    2 cups water — prefer purified or distilled

Directions:

1. Place almonds in blender and grind to a fine powder. Add 1 cup water and blend. Add additional cup of water and blend to form a smooth milk. One to two teaspoons of sweetener can be added for taste.
2. Blanched almonds produce a whiter and smoother beverage. Almonds can be blanched by placing them in 1 cup boiling water. Allow them to stand in the water until the skin easily slips off. Remove skins and let almonds dry before proceeding in above directions.
3. Wholesome and Hearty has a prepackaged almond milk that is quite tasty.

Notes:

Variations:

Strawberry Milk: Use 1 cup almond milk, 1/2 cup strawberries, 1 tsp. sweetener. Blend until smooth.

Banana Milk: Use 1 cup almond milk, 1 banana. Blend until smooth. Add pinch of nutmeg and vanilla to taste.

Apple Milk: Use 1 cup fresh apple juice, 1 banana, 1 cup almond milk. Blend until smooth.

Strawberry and Banana Shake: Use 2 cups almond milk, 2 frozen bananas, 1 cup strawberries. Blend in blender until smooth. Add sweetener if desired.

Peach Shake: Use 2 cups almond milk, 2 frozen bananas, 1–2 peaches. Blend in blender until smooth. Sprinkle with cinnamon.

Banana Shake: Use 2 cups almond milk, 3 frozen bananas. Blend in blender until smooth.

Carob Chip Shake: Use 2 cups almond milk, 3 frozen bananas, 1 tbsp. carob chips. Blend in blender until smooth.

Serves 2

Nutritional Analysis:

Calories: 251 • Protein: (g) 9 • Carbs: (g) 9 • Fat: (g) 22 •
Sat. Fat: (g) 2 • Cholesterol: (mg) 0 • Fiber: (g) 5 • Sodium: (mg) 12

Notes:

LUNCHES and DINNERS

Soups:

Brown Rice and Lentil Soup
Corn Chowder
Chicken Soup
Garden Vegetable Soup
Hearty Vegetarian Chili

White Bean Chili
Lentil Soup
Potato Soup
Split Pea Soup

Vegetarian Dishes:

Zucchini Sandwich
Fried Rice
Veggie Pizza
Chili Rellenos

Easy "Pasta-less" Lasagna
Leftover Vegetable Pie
Spinach Noodle Bake
Terrific Franks

Meat Dishes
(with vegetarian options):

BBQ "Chicken"
Peanut "Chicken" Stir Fry
Savory "Chicken" Fillets
"Chicken" Salad
"Turkey" Salad

Wonderful "Halibut"
Grilled "Halibut"
Tangy "Red Snapper"
Taco Mix
"Meatloaf"

Brown Rice and Lentil Soup

A tasty and simple dinner.

1 1/2 tbsp. canola oil
2 med. onions, fresh, chopped
4 cloves garlic, fresh, minced

----

2 whole carrots, fresh, chopped
2 stalks celery, fresh, chopped

3/4 cup lentils, uncooked
2/3 cup rice, brown, medium-grain, uncooked
1/3 cup millet, uncooked
1 28–oz. can tomatoes, crushed
2 cans chicken broth, low-fat — or stock
1 tbsp. miso
1/2 tsp. basil, ground
1/2 tsp. oregano, ground
1/2 tsp. thyme, ground
1/3 cup parsley, fresh, chopped
2 tbsp. vinegar, cider
2 tsp. tamari

Directions:

1. Sauté onion and garlic in oil (or stock).
2. Add carrots and celery.
3. Add remaining ingredients.
4. Can be cooked in a crockpot all day.

Notes:

Preparation Option:
Can also be prepared in a pressure cooker. Heat to five pounds of
pressure and process for 25 minutes. If using a pressure cooker,

add the parsley, vinegar and tamari after the pressurized processing. Let simmer for an additional 15 minutes.

Serving Suggestion:

A wonderful way to serve this soup is in a Bread Bowl. Make a regular recipe of bread. Shape a thin layer over a greased oven–proof bowl. Bake for about 10 to 15 minutes. Remove bowl and bake the bread insides for about 5 minutes. Brush with olive oil and fill with hot soup. After serving the soup, tear the bread bowl apart and serve with the soup.

Menu Options:

Quick Menu Idea:
Veggie Sticks
Humus (recipe in LFH cookbook)

Company Menu Idea:
Warm Wilted Spinach Salad
Apple Cinnamon Muffins
Almond Crunch Bars

Your Favorite Menu Idea:

 Freezes well.

Serves 8

Nutritional Analysis:

Calories: 228 • Protein: (g) 10 • Carbs: (g) 39 • Fat: (g) 4 •
Sat. Fat: (g) 16 • Cholesterol: (mg) 0 • Fiber: (g) 9 • Sodium: (mg) 455

Corn Chowder

A simple soup with lots of flavor.

1/2 med. onion, fresh, chopped
1 clove garlic, fresh, minced
1 tsp. olive oil — or stock

1/2 cup celery, fresh, chopped
1/2 cup potatoes, with skin, chopped

----

1 cup corn, yellow, cut — fresh or frozen
1/2 cup carrots, fresh, grated
2 cups milk, skim — or soy, rice or almond milk

1/2 tsp. salt, sea — or tamari or Vege Sal
1/4 cup parsley, dried

Directions:

1. Sauté onion and garlic in oil or stock.
2. Add celery and potatoes and sauté a few minutes.
3. Add corn, carrots and milk. Simmer until veggies are tender.
4. Add salt to taste. Sprinkle with parsley.

Notes:

Variation:

Instead of milk, use 1 cup tomato sauce and 1 cup veggie or chicken stock. This makes a "Manhattan" based chowder.

Menu Options:

Quick Menu Idea:

Add low–fat bean dip, baked chips and a salad.

Company Menu Idea:
Cole Slaw
Zucchini Sandwiches
Packaged Cookies
Peppermint Tea

Your Favorite Menu Idea:

 Freezes well.

Serves 4

Nutritional Analysis:

Calories: 139 • Protein: (g) 7 • Carbs: (g) 25 • Fat: (g) 2 •
Sat. Fat: (g) 0 • Cholesterol: (mg) 3 • Fiber: (g) 2 • Sodium: (mg) 395

Chicken Soup

An easy chicken soup for lunches and quick meals. Make extra and freeze.

4 cups rich chicken broth
Seasoning to taste
Noodles or rice, if not food combining — or omit meat and use the noodles or rice

----

1 carrot, grated — optional

----

1 cup peas — optional
1 tbsp. white miso

Cooked chicken meat, diced

Directions:

1. Heat broth to boiling.
2. Cook noodles or rice, if using, in broth.
3. Add carrot and simmer.
4. Add miso and peas.
5. Stir in meat, if using, and heat.

Notes:

Menu Options:

Quick Menu Idea:

Crackers

Company Menu Idea:

Tossed Salad
Apple Pie

Your Favorite Menu Idea:

 Freezes well.

Serves 4

Nutritional Analysis:

Calories: 461 • Protein: (g) 31 • Carbs: (g) 65 • Fat: (g) 11 •
Sat. Fat: (g) 3 • Cholesterol: (mg) 66 • Fiber: (g) 9 • Sodium: (mg) 413

Garden Vegetable Soup

This is a wonderful soup with or without the meat. It can be made in the crockpot. It freezes well.

4   cups vegetable stock (from recipe) — or from veggie cube
1   10–oz. pkg. peas, green, frozen
10 whole mushrooms, fresh, sliced
6   stalks celery, fresh, chopped
3   med. zucchini, fresh, chopped
1   med. onion, fresh, chopped
28 oz. tomato puree (Muir Crushed)
1/4 cup parsley, dried
1   tsp. marjoram, dried
1   tsp. basil, dried leaf
1   whole bay leaf

Directions:

Place all ingredients into crockpot and cook on medium all day.
Add water if desired. Adjust seasoning, if desired.

Notes:

Ingredient Option:

Potatoes and corn can be added. Add more liquid, as needed.

Wild Game or Beef Variation:

1. Cook 1 three–pound roast in 1 quart of Knudsen Very Veggie juice all day in crock pot.
2. Cool and degrease stock. Substitute this stock for vegetable stock in recipe.
3. Shred or dice the meat.
4. Continue with above directions.

If using meat, it is best to omit the starchy veggies (corn and potatoes).

Menu Options:

Quick Menu Idea:
Whole Grain Bread

Company Menu Idea:
Waldorf Salad
Whole Grain Bread

Your Favorite Menu Idea:

 Freezes well.

Serves 6

Nutritional Analysis:
Calories: 128 • Protein: (g) 7 • Carbs: (g) 28 • Fat: (g) 1 •
Sat. Fat: (g) 0 • Cholesterol: (mg) 0 • Fiber: (g) 8 • Sodium: (mg) 610

Hearty Vegetarian Chili

A tasty chili, made without meat, that can be quickly tossed into a crockpot. It freezes well.

1 med. onion, fresh, chopped
1 clove garlic, fresh, minced
2 1/4 tsp. olive oil — or stock

---

1 whole carrot, fresh, chopped

---

1 15–oz. can pinto beans — prefer organic
1 15–oz. can kidney beans
1 10–oz. pkg. corn, yellow, frozen — or fresh
2 tsp. cumin, ground
1 tsp. Parsley Patch Mexican spice
1/2 tsp. Vege Sal — or sea salt to taste

Directions:

1. If time permits, sauté garlic and onion in olive oil or stock.
2. Add carrot and sauté.
3. Stir in remaining ingredients and simmer in crockpot on low or in pot until veggies are tender.
4. To make a thicker chili, stir 4 tbsp. of corn masa (corn flour) into water. Stir into soup until dissolved.
5. Cook for 10 to 15 minutes or until "raw" taste is gone.

Notes:

Variation:

Black Bean Chili:

Substitute 1 15–oz. can black beans for the kidney beans. Add 1 4–oz. can mild (or spicy) chopped green chilies.

Menu Options:

Quick Menu Idea:
Salsa and Corn Chips

Company Menu Idea:
Salsa and Corn Chips
Rice Pudding (homemade or Lundberg)

Your Favorite Menu Idea:

 Freezes well.

Serves 8

Nutritional Analysis:
Calories: 124 • Protein: (g) 6 • Carbs: (g) 23 • Fat: (g) 15 •
Sat. Fat: (g) 0 • Cholesterol: (mg) 0 • Fiber: (g) 3 • Sodium: (mg) 349

White Bean Chili

An easy chili with a twist of color.

1 med. onion, fresh, chopped
1 clove garlic, fresh, minced
2 tsp. olive oil — or stock
----
4 oz. green chili peppers, canned, diced
1/2 tsp. cumin, ground
1/2 tsp. oregano, dried leaf
1/2 tsp. Parsley Patch Mexican spice — or to taste
1/2 tsp. Vege Sal — or to taste

3/4 cup vegetable stock (from recipe) — or from veggie cubes
4 cups navy beans, canned — or 2 cans

Directions:

1. Sauté onion and garlic in oil or stock.
2. Add chilies and seasonings and sauté for a couple of minutes.
3. Stir in beans and stock and simmer until heated. Add more liquid, if needed. Adjust seasoning, if desired.

Notes:

Menu Options:

Quick Menu Idea:
Whole Grain Muffin or Bread Stick
Carrot Sticks
Company Menu Idea:
Raw Veggie Platter with Red Pepper Dip (LFH cookbook)
Oat Pecan Muffins

Your Favorite Menu Idea:

 Freezes well.

Serves 4

Nutritional Analysis:
Calories: 332 • Protein: (g) 20 • Carbs: (g) 57 • Fat: (g) 4 •
Sat. Fat: (g) 1 • Cholesterol: (mg) 0 • Fiber: (g) 14 • Sodium: (mg) 1375

Lentil Soup

This is a favorite from our Lifestyle for Health cookbook. It can be cooked in a crockpot and it freezes well.

1   med. onion, fresh, chopped
1   clove garlic, fresh, minced
2   tsp. olive oil — or stock

----

2   whole carrots, fresh, chopped

----

6   cups vegetable stock (from recipe) — or water
1   16–oz. can tomatoes (Muir crushed)
2   cups lentils, uncooked
2   tbsp. molasses, blackstrap — or to taste (omit)
1/2 tsp. basil, dried leaf
1/2 tsp. salt, sea — or San J tamari
1/4 tsp. thyme, dried leaf and sage

Directions:

1. If time permits, sauté onion and garlic in oil or stock.
2. Add carrots and sauté.
3. Stir in all ingredients in pot or crockpot and cook until tender. Adjust seasoning as desired.

Notes:

Menu Options:

Quick Menu Idea:

Veggie Sticks
Humus (recipe in LFH cookbook)

Company Menu Idea:
Warm Wilted Spinach Salad
Apple Cinnamon Muffins
Almond Crunch Bars

Your Favorite Menu Idea:

 Freezes well.

Serves 6

Nutritional Analysis:

Calories: 268 • Protein: (g) 16 • Carbs: (g) 46 • Fat: (g) 3 •
Sat. Fat: (g) 0 • Cholesterol: (mg) 0 • Fiber: (g) 21 • Sodium: (mg) 341

Potato Soup

This is an easy soup that is wonderful in the winter. Try the different variations or add a few of your own.

4 med. potatoes, with skin, diced
2 whole carrots, fresh, diced

----

1 med. onion, fresh, chopped
1 clove garlic, fresh, minced
1 tsp. olive oil — or stock

----

3 cups milk, skim — or rice milk or soy
1 oz. cheddar cheese, sharp — soy or almond cheddar
1 tbsp. parsley, dried
1/2 tsp. tamari — San J, to taste

Directions:

1. Cook potatoes and carrots in water to cover.
2. Sauté onion and garlic in oil or stock.
3. Add onion mixture to veggies. Puree in blender with enough water to make a smooth mixture.
4. Return to pan and add milk, cheese, parsley and enough seasonings to taste. Do not let boil. Thin with more milk, if desired.

Notes:

Variations:

Vichyssoises:

Substitute 5 tbsp. minced fresh mushrooms for the carrots. Cook and blend according to the directions and cool. Chill thoroughly and serve with a garnish of chopped chives.

Broccoli Potato Soup:

Add 1 cup fresh, chopped broccoli to potato mixture. Cooked leftover broccoli can be added to the puree step.

Menu Options:

Quick Menu Idea:
Whole Grain Muffins or Bread
Tossed Salad.

Company Menu Idea:
Tossed Spinach Salad
Oat Pecan Muffins
Apple Cherry Crisp

Your Favorite Menu Idea:

Serves 4

Nutritional Analysis:

Calories: 343 • Protein: (g) 14 • Carbs: (g) 63 • Fat: (g) 4 •
Sat. Fat: (g) 2 • Cholesterol: (mg) 11 • Fiber: (g) 6 • Sodium: (mg) 218

Split Pea Soup

This is an easy soup to prepare the night before during dinner or in the morning in a crockpot. It freezes and reheats well.

1 med. onion, fresh, chopped
2 tsp. olive oil — or stock

----

1 stalk celery, fresh, chopped
1 whole carrot, fresh, chopped

----

2 cups split peas, uncooked — or 1 pound
1/2 tsp. celery seed — or celery salt
1 tbsp. miso, white

Directions:

1. Sauté onion in oil.
2. Add celery and carrot and sauté.
3. Add remaining ingredients and cook until tender in pan, crockpot or pressure cooker.

Notes:

Variation:

Miso can be replaced with a veggie bouillon cube (be sure there is no MSG).

Menu Options:

Quick Menu Idea:

Tossed Salad
Baked Corn Chips

Company Menu Idea:

Cole Slaw or Tossed Salad
Oven Baked French Fries
Cornbread

Your Favorite Menu Ideas:

 Freezes well.

Serves 4

Nutritional Analysis:

Calories: 380 • Protein: (g) 25 • Carbs: (g) 64 • Fat: (g) 4 •
Sat. Fat: (g) 1 • Cholesterol: (mg) 0 • Fiber: (g) 26 • Sodium: (mg) 188

Zucchini Sandwich

A delicious and easy sandwich that even pleases "zucchini haters." A great way to use an abundance of summer zucchini.

2 tsp. olive oil — or stock
1/2 med. onion, fresh, chopped
1 clove garlic, fresh, minced

----

2 cups zucchini, fresh, chopped or sliced thin
1/4 cup carrots, fresh, grated
1 tsp. Italian herbs

----

3 whole hamburger buns (half for each sandwich)
1 med. tomato, fresh, sliced thin
1/4 cup parmesan cheese, fresh grated — or soy parmesan

Directions:

1. Sauté onion and garlic in oil or stock.
2. Stir in zucchini, carrots and herbs. Cook until tender.
3. Place zucchini mixture on half of bun. Top with tomato slice and cheese.
4. Broil until cheese is lightly browned.

Notes:

Ingredient Substitution:

Pizza sauce can replace the tomatoes. Place it on bun before the zucchini mixture.

Menu Options:
Quick Menu Idea:
Com Chowder

Company Menu Idea:
Gazpacho (LFH cookbook)
Oven Baked French Fries
Packaged Cookies

Your Favorite Menu Idea:

Serves 6

Nutritional Analysis:
Calories: 64 • Protein: (g) 3 • Carbs: (g) 7 • Fat: (g) 3 •
Sat. Fat: (g) 1 • Cholesterol: (mg) 2 • Fiber: (g) 1 • Sodium: (mg) 102

Fried Rice

A family favorite we have on a regular basis. Make a big pot of rice on Monday, chill it and be ready for many rice dishes.

1 med. onion, fresh, chopped
1 clove garlic, fresh, minced
1 tbsp. olive oil

----

4 cups rice, brown, medium grain, cooked, cold
2 tbsp. tamari
1 10–oz. pkg. peas, green, frozen
1/4 cup carrots, fresh, grated
3/4 cup bean sprouts, fresh

Directions:

1. Sauté onion and garlic in oil on low for 15 to 30 minutes. The longer the sautéing, the sweeter the flavor.
2. Add the peas and carrots, and cook until tender.
3. Stir in the rice, sprouts and enough tamari to add color and flavor.

Notes:

Ingredient Option:

Sliced mushrooms may also be added during the sauté stage.

Menu Options:

Quick Menu Idea:

Tossed Salad

Company Menu Idea:

Homemade or Purchased Egg Rolls
Stir Fried Veggies
Rich Bars

Your Favorite Menu Idea:

Serves 6

Nutritional Analysis:

Calories: 212 • Protein: (g) 6 • Carbs: (g) 39 • Fat: (g) 3 •
Sat. Fat: (g) 1 • Cholesterol: (mg) 0 • Fiber: (g) 3 • Sodium: (mg) 376

Veggie Pizza

A delicious pizza. Use purchased pizza crust or homemade crust — with or without yeast.

1/4 15–oz. can tomato sauce with mushrooms and peppers — or pizza sauce

---

1/2 10–oz. bag spinach, fresh, chopped
4 whole mushrooms, fresh, sliced
1/2 med. onion, fresh, sliced thin
1/2 whole pepper, green, fresh — slivered or sliced
1/2 cup broccoli, fresh, chopped

1/2 cup mozzarella cheese, part skim, grated

---

1 whole pizza crust, homemade

Directions:

1. Spread sauce on pre–baked pizza crust.
2. Place a layer of spinach on crust.
3. Add veggies onto spinach (add any other desired veggies).
4. Sprinkle with cheese.
5. Bake at 425 degrees for 7 to 8 minutes or until done.

Notes:

Preparation Option:

A pizza stone will produce a nice crispy crust. Using a pizza paddle or peel, slip the prepared pizza onto the preheated stone. Bake as directed.

Menu Options:

Quick Menu Idea:
Tossed Salad
Mint Tea

Company Menu Idea:
Veggie Tray with Dip
Carrot Mini Cakes

Your Favorite Menu Idea:

 Freezes well. Pizza crusts can be partially baked (4 to 5 minutes), and frozen to use as a Boboli–type crust. Or, pizza can be assembled and frozen. Bake either crust or finished pizza from frozen state until done.

Serves 4

Nutritional Analysis:

Calories: 309 • Protein: (g) 15 • Carbs: (g) 53 • Fat: (g) 7 •
Sat. Fat: (g) 19 • Cholesterol: (mg) 7 • Fiber: (g) 3 • Sodium: (mg) 231

Chili Rellenos

A delicious dish that has become a family favorite.

2 cups refried beans, canned, vegetarian — or homemade from recipe
1 3.5-oz. can chile peppers, green, mild, diced
5 1/3 oz. Monterey Jack cheese, low–fat, grated
1 1/2 cups rice, brown, short–grain, cooked
2 cups enchilada sauce (from recipe) — or canned

----

1 10-oz. pkg. corn, yellow, frozen, cooked — optional
2 cups lettuce, green leaf, chopped — optional
2 oz. corn chips, plain, baked — optional

Directions:

1. Oil 9" square dish. Place beans in bottom.
2. Place chiles on top of beans and cover with cheese. Cover with thin layer of rice. Cover with sauce.
3. Bake at 350 degrees for 25 to 30 minutes.
4. Serve with shredded lettuce and corn chips. A little cooked corn and a drizzle of honey also add a nice touch.

Notes:

Menu Options:

Quick Menu Idea:
Greens
Salsa and Chips

Company Menu Idea:
Tex–Mex Corn
Lettuce
Chips

Your Favorite Menu Idea:

 Freezes well. Freeze prior to baking the casserole.

Serves 6

Nutritional Analysis:

Calories: 369 • Protein: (g) 18 • Carbs: (g) 50 • Fat: (g) 12 •
Sat. Fat: (g) 1 • Cholesterol: (mg) 118 • Fiber: (g) 7 • Sodium: (mg) 1257

Easy "Pasta–less" Lasagna

The fastest lasagna in the world. Not only is it meatless, it also has no pasta.

1   whole eggplant, fresh, sliced 1/2" thick

---

1   med. zucchini, fresh, sliced
1   whole pepper, red, fresh, seeded and sliced
7   whole mushrooms, fresh, sliced
3 1/4   small tomatoes, fresh, Italian, sliced
3   oz. mozzarella cheese, part skim, thin slices — or grated
1   15–oz. jar marinara sauce, fat–free
— or homemade

1/4   cup parmesan cheese, fresh grated

Directions:

1. Broil eggplant for 10 to 12 minutes or until limp. This can be done in advance.
2. Place 1/2 cup pasta sauce in prepared 11" x 7" pan.
3. Layer half of eggplant, zucchini, peppers, mushrooms, tomatoes, mozzarella and sauce. Repeat layers.
4. Sprinkle with parmesan. Bake at 375 degrees for 25 to 30 minutes or until hot throughout.

Notes:

Time Saver Tip:

This can be prepared the night before or the morning of the meal.

Menu Options:

Quick Menu Idea:
Tossed Salad
Whole Grain Bread

Company Menu Idea:
Warm Wilted Spinach Salad
Bagel Chips (purchased)
Chocolate Mousse (LFH cookbook)

Your Favorite Menu Idea:

 Freezes well. Best frozen after baking. Thaw or bake frozen.

Serves 5

Nutritional Analysis:

Calories: 143 • Protein: (g) 10 • Carbs: (g) 17 • Fat: (g) 4 •
Sat. Fat: (g) 3 • Cholesterol: (mg) 12 • Fiber: (g) 4 • Sodium: (mg) 401

Leftover Vegetable Pie

A great way to use leftover veggies. Each time it will be a new flavor sensation.

1 med. onion, fresh, chopped
1 clove garlic, fresh, minced

---

3 cups broccoli, cooked — or 3–4 cups cooked mixed veggies
1 1/2 med. tomatoes, fresh, cut in small wedges

---

1 9" pie crust, frozen — or homemade

1/4 cup Monterey Jack cheese, low–fat, shredded

Directions:

1. Sauté onion and garlic in stock or water, if time permits.
2. Combine veggies, tomatoes, onions and garlic.
3. Prick bottom and sides of crust. Place veggie mixture in pie shell.
4. Top with cheese. Bake at 375 degrees for about 25 minutes.

Notes:

Time Saver Tip:

This can be prepared in advance and refrigerated.

Menu Options:

Quick Menu Idea:

Tossed Salad

Company Menu Idea:

Mashed Sweet Potatoes or Squash
Tossed Salad
Fudgy Brownies

Your Favorite Menu Idea:

Serves 4

Nutritional Analysis:
Calories: 224 • Protein: (g) 7 • Carbs: (g) 26 • Fat: (g) 12 •
Sat. Fat: (g) 4 • Cholesterol: (mg) 3 • Fiber: (g) 4 • Sodium: (mg) 250

Spinach Noodle Bake

An easy pasta meal that bakes by itself in the oven. Check out the dairy–free option.

8 oz. cottage cheese, low–fat, 1% fat
1 pkg. Mori Nu "lite" tofu, firm

----

1 10–oz. pkg. spinach, frozen leaf, thawed, drained
8 oz. pasta, lasagna, spelt, dry, cooked, drained
1 15–oz. jar marinara sauce, fat-free — prefer Muir
1/4 cup parmesan cheese, fresh grated — optional

Directions:

1. Blend tofu and cottage cheese in blender until smooth.
2. Layer small amount of sauce in 9" x 7" prepared pan. Add one half of noodles, spinach, tofu and sauce. Repeat layers.
3. Sprinkle top with parmesan, if desired.

Notes:

Variation:

Fresh, steamed, chopped spinach can be used.

Ingredient Substitution:

Replace cottage cheese with:

1 pkg. Mori Nu "lite" tofu, firm
2 tbsp. olive oil
1/4 tsp. nutmeg
1/4 tsp. sea salt

Blend in blender until smooth. Add the remaining pkg. of tofu in the recipe and blend until smooth.

If soy is not tolerated, replace the one pkg. of tofu with 2 eggs or 3 egg whites or EGG SUBSTITUTE equal to 2 eggs.

Menu Options:

Quick Menu Idea:
Steamed Broccoli
Whole Grain Bread

Company Menu Idea:
Green and Red Zucchini
Green Onion Biscuits

Your Favorite Menu Idea:

 Freezes well. Freeze before, or after, baking.

Serves 5

Nutritional Analysis:
Calories: 250 • Protein: (g) 18 • Carbs: (g) 35 • Fat: (g) 4 •
Sat. Fat: (g) 1 • Cholesterol: (mg) 38 • Fiber: (g) 19 • Sodium: (mg) 588

Terrific Franks

These treats make great snacks or quick and easy meals. The tofu dogs make this a simple vegetarian dish.

1   cup cornmeal, whole–grain, yellow — or baking mix
3/4   8–oz. cup yogurt, plain, low–fat — or soft tofu
1/2   cup soy milk — or rice or almond milk
1   tbsp. canola oil

----
4   whole tofu hot dogs, plain, cut into sixths
----
1   tbsp. sesame seeds, hulled — optional

Directions:

1.   Mix cornmeal baking mix with yogurt, milk and oil.
2.   Line muffin tins with paper or oil.
3.   Fill muffin tins 1/2 full. Place 1 to 2 hot dog slices in each tin.
4.   Sprinkle with seeds. Bake at 400 degrees about 20 minutes or until done.

Notes:

Ingredient Substitution:

Turkey dogs could be used in place of tofu hot dogs. Tofu dogs can be lower in fat.

Variations:

Replace cornmeal baking mix, yogurt, milk and oil with:

1/2 cup cornmeal
1/2 cup flour (barley or whole wheat or spelt)
1 tbsp. baking powder
1/2 tsp. salt
1 egg — or EGG SUBSTITUTE
1 cup milk
1/4 cup sweetener — granular or liquid

Meals in 30 Minutes

Mix dry ingredients. Mix liquid ingredients. Combine. Proceed by placing batter in muffin tins.

Menu Options:

Quick Menu Idea:
Carrot Sticks
Packaged Cookies

Company Menu Idea:
Sweet Carrots
Steamed Broccoli
Iced Mint Tea

Your Favorite Menu Idea:

 Freezes well after baking. Thaw and reheat, or reheat from frozen state.

Makes 10–12 muffins
Serves 9

Nutritional Analysis:
Calories: 192 • Protein: (g) 7 • Carbs: (g) 20 • Fat: (g) 10 •
Sat. Fat: (g) 3 • Cholesterol: (mg) 21 • Fiber: (g) 1 • Sodium: (mg) 318

BBQ "Chicken"

A wonderful BBQ delight that is quick and easy. Check out the variations.

   1 lb. chicken, breast wo/skin
   2/3 cup barbecue sauce — Annie's is preferred

Directions:

1. Steam chicken until tender.
2. Shred chicken and stir in desired amount of BBQ sauce.

Notes:

Ingredient Variation:

Turkey fillet

Whole Chicken, to bake:

Place 1/4 onion, sea salt, fresh thyme and basil inside chicken cavity. Bake chicken at 375 degrees for about 1 to 1 1/2 hours, basting with natural juice every 10 to 15 minutes. Baste with sauce the last 30 minutes. This takes a little longer but is sensational. Do 2 or 3 at the same time and freeze.

Vegetarian Options:

Use tempeh and grill or broil, brushing with BBQ sauce until heated through.

Menu Options:

Quick Menu Idea:
Tossed Salad
Steamed Broccoli

Company Menu Idea:
Tossed Salad
Red Pepper Boats
Chocolate Mousse (LFH cookbook)

Your Favorite Menu Idea:

 Both the chicken and vegetarian versions freeze well.
Freeze in individual serving size containers.

Serves 4

Nutritional Analysis:

Calories: 53 • Protein: (g) 5 • Carbs: (g) 5 • Fat: (g) 1 •
Sat. Fat: (g) 0 • Cholesterol: (mg) 11 • Fiber: (g) 1 • Sodium: (mg) 349

Peanut "Chicken" Stir Fry

An exotic yet simple dish that utilizes cucumbers in a stir fry.

1 lb. chicken, breast wo/skin

---

1 med. onion, fresh, halved, sliced
2 cloves garlic, fresh, minced
1 whole pepper, red, fresh, cut in match stick pieces
2 whole cucumbers, unpeeled, cut into half moons
10 tbsp. San J Thai peanut sauce

---

2 tbsp. peanuts, dry–roasted, unsalted

Directions:

1. Skin and debone chicken. Cut into bite size chunks.
2. Stir fry onion and garlic until translucent.
3. Add chicken and cook, stirring, until chicken turns white. Add peanut sauce and bring to a boil. Stir in pepper and cook about 1 minute. Add cucumber and stir to coat. May be garnished with ground peanuts, if desired.

Notes:

Vegetarian Options:

Use crumbled tempeh or chicken flavored seitan in place of the chicken.

Menu Options:

Quick Menu Idea:
Brown Rice

Company Menu Idea:
Brown Rice
Egg Rolls (LFH Cookbook)
Chinese Tea

Your Favorite Menu Idea:

Serves 6

Nutritional Analysis:

Calories: 59 • Protein: (g) 5 • Carbs: (g) 6 • Fat: (g) 2 •
Sat. Fat: (g) 0 • Cholesterol: (mg) 7 • Fiber: (g) 2 • Sodium: (mg) 9

Savory "Chicken" Fillets

A quick way to prepare chicken breasts without sacrificing flavor. Be sure to check out the vegetarian option.

    1 lb. chicken, breast wo/skin
    1/4 cup vegetable broth
    1 1/2 tsp. Parsley Patch Dill seasoning — or garlic seasoning
    1 tbsp. lemon juice, fresh — or to taste

Directions:

1. Sauté chicken in stock about 5 to 7 minutes or until lightly browned.
2. Sprinkle with Parsley Patch. Squeeze fresh lemon juice over top.
3. Turn chicken over and repeat process. Cook until done.
4. Sprinkle with freshly minced parsley.

Notes:

Ingredient Options:

Turkey fillets can be used.

Vegetarian Options:

Tofu steaks (see chicken alternatives in appendix) or seitan can be used.

Menu Options:

Quick Menu Idea:

Tex–Mex Corn
Tossed Salad

Company Idea:
Warm Wilted Spinach Salad
Baked Butternut Squash, mashed
Carob Brownies

Your Favorite Menu Idea:

 Freezes well. This can be frozen before or after cooking. Both the chicken and vegetarian versions can be frozen.

Serves 4

Nutritional Analysis:

Calories: 24 • Protein: (g) 4 • Carbs: (g) 1 • Fat: (g) 1 •
Sat. Fat: (g) 0 • Cholesterol: (mg) 11 • Fiber: (g) 0 • Sodium: (mg) 67

"Chicken" Salad

A hot chicken mixture that can be placed over cool, crisp lettuce greens. Check out the vegetarian options.

1 lb. chicken, breast wo/skin, cut into 1/4" strips
2 tsp. olive oil — or stock

---

1 cup mushrooms, fresh, sliced

1/4 cup almonds, slivered — or walnuts, optional
2 tbsp. Italian salad dressing, diet — or Annie's Raspberry Dressing
2 1/2 cups lettuce, mixed greens, prepackaged

Directions:

1. Sauté or stir fry chicken in oil or stock.
2. Stir in mushrooms and cook until tender.
3. Stir in nuts and barely toast. (Can be toasted in oven while chicken is cooking for more flavor, 350 degrees for about 10 minutes.)
4. Stir in dressing and place on top of lettuce greens.

Notes:

Vegetarian Options:

Use crumbled tempeh in place of chicken.
Use seitan in place of chicken.

Ingredient Substitution:

Pinon nuts for almonds

Menu Options:

Quick Menu Idea:
Raw Veggie Platter

Company Menu Idea:
Raw Veggie Platter
Oat Pecan Muffins
Blueberry Cheesecake Bars

Your Favorite Menu Idea:

Serves 5

Nutritional Analysis:

Calories: 105 • Protein: (g) 6 • Carbs: (g) 5 • Fat: (g) 7 •
Sat. Fat: (g) 1 • Cholesterol: (mg) 9 • Fiber: (g) 3 • Sodium: (mg) 128

"Turkey Salad"

An elegant, quick salad. Marinade the meat overnight and be ready to grill or broil the next night.

2 tbsp. honey
1 tbsp. tamari — or "lite"
1 tsp. ginger root, grated, raw — or 1/4 tsp. ground
1 clove garlic, fresh, minced
1 lb. turkey breast tenderloins

1/4 cup Italian dressing (from recipe) — or favorite dressing

---

3 whole green onions, sliced
1 tbsp. red pepper, whole, in rings
1 cup green peppers, fresh, whole, julienned
1/4 cup almonds, slivered — optional
6 cups lettuce, mixed greens, prepackaged

Directions:

1. Mix marinate ingredients. Place turkey into marinade and let set overnight.
2. Toss salad ingredients together.
3. Grill or broil turkey. Slice into 1/4" slices.
4. Toss turkey and salad with dressing.

Notes:

Ingredient Variation:

Chicken breast can be used in place of turkey.

Vegetarian Options:

Tofu or tempeh can replace turkey.

Dressing:

   1 clove garlic
   1/2" of fresh ginger
   1 tbsp. fresh parsley
   3 tbsp. rice vinegar
   5 tbsp. almond butter
   1 tbsp. tamari
   3 tsp. hoisin sauce, optional
   3 tsp. sesame oil

Blend all ingredients in blender. Chill. Use in place of bottled dressing, as needed.

Menu Options:

Quick Menu Idea:

Bagel Chips (purchased)

Company Menu Idea:

Bagel Chips (purchased)
Orange Parfait (LFH cookbook, use firm tofu instead of soft for a mousse–like consistency)

Your Favorite Menu Idea:

Serves 6

Nutritional Analysis:

Calories: 170 • Protein: (g) 10 • Carbs: (g) 15 • Fat: (g) 9 •
Sat. Fat: (g) 1 • Cholesterol: (mg) 14 • Fiber: (g) 6 • Sodium: (mg) 332

Wonderful "Halibut"

A tasty, easy meal.

> 3/4 cup tamari
> 3/4 cup orange juice, fresh
> 2 cloves garlic, fresh, minced
>
> --
>
> 2 lb. halibut

Directions:

1. Combine tamari, juice and garlic. MARINATE halibut steaks in marinade for about 2 hours.
2. Bake the steaks in the marinade at 350 degrees until flaky.

Notes:

Vegetarian Option:

Marinate tofu that has been cut into 1" chunks. Bake or stir fry the chunks.

Menu Options:

Quick Menu Idea:

Spinach Salad with Poppy Seed Dressing
Sliced Tomatoes

Company Menu Idea:

Rice Salad
Green Onion Biscuits
Almond Crunch Bars

Your Favorite Menu Idea:

 Freezes well. Both the chicken and vegetarian versions can be frozen before or after cooking.

Serves 4

Nutritional Analysis:

Calories: 151 • Protein: (g) 13 • Carbs: (g) 8 • Fat: (g) 8 •
Sat. Fat: (g) 1 • Cholesterol: (mg) 25 • Fiber: (g) 1 • Sodium: (mg) 2474

Grilled "Halibut"

A nearly fat–free way to serve fresh fish.

4 fillets halibut — skinless
1 large lemon, thin slices

1/4 cup tofu, low–fat, crumbled
4   green onions — chopped
1 tsp. ginger root grated — or 1/2 tsp. powdered
1 clove garlic, fresh, chopped
2 tbsp. mustard, stone ground
2 tbsp. parsley, dried
1 tbsp. vinegar, cider — or flavored
1 tbsp. lemon juice, fresh

Directions:

1. Place lemon slices on top of fish. Broil or grill until done.
2. Place all remaining ingredients in blender and blend.
3. Serve fish with sauce. Garnish with parsley or slivered spinach.

Notes:

Ingredient Option:

Use chicken breast for fish.

Vegetarian Options:

Use tofu, seitan or tempeh for chicken.

Menu Options:

Quick Menu Idea:

Corn on the Cob
Cole Slaw

Company Menu Idea:
Peachy Carrots (LFH cookbook)
Spinach Salad (LFH cookbook)
Cornmeal Muffins (LFH cookbook)

Your Favorite Menu Idea:

Serves 6

Nutritional Analysis:
Calories: 319 • Protein: (g) 58 • Carbs: (g) 3 • Fat: (g) 7 •
Sat. Fat: (g) 1 • Cholesterol: (mg) 87 • Fiber: (g) 1 • Sodium: (mg) 214

Tangy "Red Snapper"

Quick and easy does it.

3 fillets snapper, mixed species — or 6 servings

----

1 tbsp. olive oil — or stock
1/4 cup orange juice, fresh
1 tbsp. tamari — or "lite"
1/4 tsp. nutmeg, ground — or less
1/4 tsp. cayenne pepper — or less

Directions:

1. Wash fish and pat dry.
2. Combine all remaining ingredients in jar and blend.
3. Pour over fish. Bake fish at 350 degrees for 20 minutes or until fish flakes easily.

Notes:

Ingredient Option:

Chicken can replace fish.

Vegetarian Options:

Tofu or tempeh can be used instead of fish.

Menu Options:

Quick Menu Idea:

Steamed Asparagus
Tossed Salad

Company Menu Idea:

Asparagus and Pecans
Waldorf Salad
Baked Rice Pilaf (LFH cookbook)

Your Favorite Menu Idea:

Serves 6

Nutritional Analysis:

Calories: 136 • Protein: (g) 23 • Carbs: (g) 1 • Fat: (g) 4 •
Sat. Fat: (g) 1 • Cholesterol: (mg) 40 • Fiber: (g) 0 • Sodium: (mg) 216

Lunches and Dinners: Meat Dishes

Taco Mix

A great seasoning mix to use with ground turkey or TVP. *

- 1 tbsp. onion flakes, dried
- 1 1/2 tsp. chili pepper — or powder
- 2 tsp. cumin, ground
- 1/2 tsp. salt, sea
- 1/4 tsp. red pepper, flakes
- 1/4 tsp. garlic powder
- 1/2 tsp. arrowroot powder
- 1/4 tsp. oregano, dried leaf

Directions:

1. Mix all ingredients together.
2. Brown 1 pound of meat or TVP.
3. Add spice mixture and blend well.
4. Add 1 tbsp. natural ketchup and 1/2 cup water. Simmer for about 10 minutes or until thickened.
5. Serve in taco shells with trimmings or with greens in a taco salad.

Notes: *1 recipe makes: 3 TBSP plus 1 tsp.*

Vegetarian Option:

* TVP, or Texturized Vegetable Protein, a soy–based meat extender found in health food stores, can replace ground turkey.

Menu Options:

Quick Menu Idea:

Lettuce and Taco Fixings

Company Menu Idea:

Taco Fixings
Tex–Mex Corn
Apple Cherry Crisp

Your Favorite Menu Idea:

Enough for 8 to 10 tacos

Nutritional Analysis:

Calories: 10 • Protein: (g) 0 • Carbs: (g) 2 • Fat: (g) 0 •
Sat. Fat: (g) 0 • Cholesterol: (mg) 0 • Fiber: (g) 0 • Sodium: (mg) 202

"Meatloaf"

Good for those wanting a hearty meatloaf with a healthy edge.

1/2 cup red onion, sweet, fresh, minced
3 cloves garlic, fresh, minced
2 tsp. canola oil

3/4 cup celery, fresh, minced
1/2 cup carrot, fresh, minced
1/3 cup pepper, red, fresh, minced
1/3 large pepper, yellow, fresh, minced
1/3 cup green pepper, fresh, minced
3/4 cup green onion, minced

----

1 tsp. tamari
1/4 tsp. cayenne pepper
1/2 tsp. cumin, ground
1/2 tsp. nutmeg, ground
1/2 cup tomato sauce
2 lb. ground beef, extra lean — Coleman
1 large egg, beaten — or EGG SUBSTITUTE
3/4 cup oats, slightly ground in blender

Directions:

1. Sauté onion and garlic in oil until tender (about 5 to 10 minutes). Add other vegetables and sauté an additional 10 minutes.
2. Stir in all seasoning. Add tomato sauce, meat, egg and oats. Mix gently.
3. Place in a large loaf pan, 2 medium loaf pans or make miniature loaves.
4. Bake at 350 degrees until done: mini loaves about 20 minutes, medium loaf about 35–40 minutes, large loaf about 50 minutes.

Serve with mushroom gravy or shallot gravy.

Notes:

Ingredient Options:

Use organic ground turkey in place of ground beef. The same kind of peppers can be used in place of the 3 colors.

Vegetarian Option:

Use 2 pounds of frozen, thawed, drained tofu that has been crumbled in place of the ground meat. Omit the egg in the vegetarian option.

Menu Options:

Quick Menu Idea:
Baked Potato
Steamed Broccoli

Company Menu Idea:
Peachy Carrots (LFH cookbook)
Steamed Green Beans
Tollhouse Cookies

Your Favorite Menu Idea:

 Freezes well. This can be made in small muffin sizes and frozen (small sizes cook more quickly). It is best cooked, frozen and reheated for bulk cooking.

Serves 8

Nutritional Analysis:

Calories: 317 • Protein: (g) 25 • Carbs: (g) 15 • Fat: (g) 17 •
Sat. Fat: (g) 6 • Cholesterol: (mg) 95 • Fiber: (g) 1 • Sodium: (mg) 217

Notes:

SIDE DISHES

Salads:

Waldorf Sald

Warm Wilted Spinach Salad

Rice Salad

Vegetables:

Asparagus and Pecans

Sweet Carrots

Green and Red Zucchini

Golden Hashbrowns

Oven Baked French Fries

Tex–Mex Corn

Savory Broccoli

Zippy Bok Choy

Stuffed Red Peppers

Grains and Breads:

Crunchy Granola

Pizza Crust

Oat Crackers

Oat Pecan Muffins

Cornbread

Cinnamon Muffins

Green Onion Biscuits

Strawberry Scones

Condiments:

French Dressing

Tahini Dip

Green Goddess Dressing

Miso Tahini Dip

Poppy Seed Dressing

Honey Butter

Mushroom Sauce

Berry Good Syrup

Desserts:

Almond Crunch Bars

Carrot Mini Cakes

Blueberry Cheesecake Bars

Apple Cherry Crisp

Rich Bars

Apple Pie

Fudgy Brownies

Waldorf Salad

A tasty treat any time of the year.

3 cups apples, fresh (3 apples)
1 1/2 tbsp. lemon juice, fresh — or to taste
1 whole orange, peeled, cut into sections
1 stalk celery, fresh, chopped
2 tbsp. pecans

1/2 cup mayo, salad dressing type, light — or Nayonaise
1/2 cup orange juice, fresh
1 tbsp. lemon juice, fresh
1 tbsp. honey — or to taste

Directions:

1. Mix apples with lemon juice to prevent discoloration.
2. Mix orange, celery and pecans with apples.
3. Mix dressing ingredients in blender until smooth. Adjust sweetness as desire. Cinnamon adds a nice touch.

Notes:

Ingredient Substitutions:

Soy mayo or Mori Nu "lite" Tofu, firm can replace the lite mayo. May need more orange juice to make into a dressing consistency.

Non–fat cottage cheese or yogurt can replace the mayo.

Ingredient Additions:

Raisins, chopped dates, sunflower or sesame seeds can be added.

This is a great side dish for any meal.
Serves 3

Nutritional Analysis:

Calories: 254 • Protein: (g) 2 • Carbs: (g) 41 • Fat: (g) 11 •
Sat. Fat: (g) 2 • Cholesterol: (mg) 10 • Fiber: (g) 5 • Sodium: (mg) 211

Meals in 30 Minutes

Rice Salad

A delicious way to use leftover rice. It can be a side dish or the star of a vegetarian meal.

> 2 1/2 cups zucchini, fresh, julienned strips
> 1 cup carrots, fresh, julienned pieces
> 2 tsp. olive oil — or stock
>
> ---
>
> 1 tsp. basil, dried leaf
> 1 tsp. thyme, dried leaf
>
> ---
>
> 2 1/2 cups rice, brown basmati, cooked
> 1/2 cup tomatoes, canned — or sundried, slivered
> 1/4 cup basil, fresh, torn — optional
>
> ---
>
> 1/2 cup Italian salad dressing, diet — or favorite vinaigrette

Directions:

1. Sauté zucchini and carrots in oil until tender.
2. Sprinkle in the herbs to heat with the veggies.
3. Stir in rice, sun-dried tomatoes and fresh basil, if using.
4. Toss with dressing. Serve over a bed of salad greens if desired.

Notes:

Ingredient Substitution:

Cooked quinoa or a wild rice blend could replace the brown rice.

Serves 4

Nutritional Analysis:

Calories: 220 • Protein: (g) 5 • Carbs: (g) 37 • Fat: (g) 7 •
Sat. Fat: (g) 1 • Cholesterol: (mg) 2 • Fiber: (g) 5 • Sodium: (mg) 303

Warm Wilted Spinach Salad

A tasty, easy salad to add zip to any meal or as a simple summer lunch.

1/2 cup tempeh (1/2 pkg.)
2 cloves garlic, fresh, minced
1/4 cup almonds, sliced
2 tsp. olive oil — or stock

----

1 tbsp. lemon juice, fresh — more, if desired
1 tbsp. vinegar, cider — or balsamic
1/4 tsp. salt, sea — or to taste

----

2 bunches spinach, fresh, leaves only, torn
2 oz. feta cheese, crumbled
1/2 cup red pepper, roasted from a jar, sliced
1/2 med. red onion, sweet, fresh, thinly sliced

Directions:

1. Sauté tempeh, garlic and almonds in oil or stock about 10 minutes.
2. Mix lemon juice, vinegar and salt.
3. Heat spinach in hot skillet with a little water until limp (this step can be omitted).
4. Toss tempeh, lemon mixture, spinach, feta, roasted red pepper and red onions.

Notes:

Preparation Option:

To roast pepper at home: Pierce pepper with fork and place directly on stove burner. Turn when outside is charred. Place in paper bag and let steam. Remove skin and seeds.

Ingredient Substitutions:

Cooked chicken strips could replace the tempeh.

Bottled dressing could replace the lemon juice mixture.

This is a great salad side dish for any meal.

Serves 4

Nutritional Analysis:

Calories: 217 • Protein: (g) 13 • Carbs: (g) 19 • Fat: (g) 13 •
Sat. Fat: (g) 4 • Cholesterol: (mg) 13 • Fiber: (g) 8 • Sodium: (mg) 421

Asparagus and Pecans

An easy vegetable dish with a twist of protein and crunch. Try the many variations.

2 lb. asparagus, tough ends removed

----

2 tbsp. apple juice, unsweetened, unfiltered — or veggie stock
1/4 cup pecans, toasted, chopped
1/4 tsp. dill weed, dried — or a pinch

Directions:

1. Steam asparagus until tender.
2. Place asparagus in baking dish. Sprinkle with apple juice, pecans and dill.
3. Bake at 350 degrees for 10 to 15 minutes or until hot.

Notes:

Ingredient Substitutions:

Use broccoli, zucchini or cauliflower in place of the asparagus.

This is a side dish for a grilled main dish or a grain dish.

Serves 5

Nutritional Analysis:

Calories: 80 • Protein: (g) 5 • Carbs: (g) 9 • Fat: (g) 4 •
Sat. Fat: (g) 0 • Cholesterol: (mg) 0 • Fiber: (g) 4 • Sodium: (mg) 20

Green and Red Zucchini

This is so very simple, yet it adds a great deal of color to your meal.

6 med. zucchini, fresh, sliced
2 med. tomatoes, fresh, sliced
1/2 med. onion, fresh, half moon slices
2 tsp. olive oil — as needed
3 tbsp. parsley, fresh, chopped
Parmesan cheese — optional

Directions:

1. Alternate layers of zucchini, tomato and onion in a prepared baking dish.
2. Drizzle with olive oil and parsley.
3. Sprinkle with parmesan (or soy parmesan) if desired. (Feta could also be used.)
4. Bake at 400 degrees for 15 to 25 minutes or until veggies are tender.

Notes:

Time Saver Tip:

This dish can bake at any temperature being used for the rest of the meal. Allow enough time for the veggies to get tender.

This is similar to a ratatouille.

Serves 4

Nutritional Analysis:

Calories: 91 • Protein: (g) 7 • Carbs: (g) 15 • Fat: (g) 3 •
Sat. Fat: (g) 1 • Cholesterol: (mg) 0 • Fiber: (g) 6 • Sodium: (mg) 19

Oven Baked French Fries

A great way to fix potatoes. Kids can help prepare and enjoy eating.

    2 large potatoes, with skin, julienned
    2 tsp. Parsley Patch Mexican spice — or garlic seasoning
    1 tsp. olive oil

Directions:

1. Toss potatoes with oil and spice seasoning.
2. Place on prepared baking sheet. Broil until browned (about 10 to 15 minutes). Flip and brown other side.

Notes:

Ingredient Substitution:

Sweet potatoes or yams can replace the potatoes. Omit the garlic seasoning. Sprinkle with nutmeg or cumin.

This is a good side dish or a main dish with a big salad.

Serves 2

Nutritional Analysis:

Calories: 372 • Protein: (g) 8 • Carbs: (g) 80 • Fat: (g) 3 •
Sat. Fat: (g) 0 • Cholesterol: (mg) 0 • Fiber: (g) 3 • Sodium: (mg) 22

Savory Broccoli

A simple, uncomplicated dish to serve with most anything.

   6 whole broccoli spears, fresh, cut in flowerets
   1 1/2 tbsp. lemon juice, fresh
   1 tbsp. canola seeds

Directions:
1. Steam broccoli until crisp tender.
2. Sprinkle with lemon juice and canola seeds.

Notes:
Ingredient Substitutions:
Replace cauliflower for all or part of the broccoli.

Sesame seeds can replace the canola seeds.

This is a good side dish when extra color is wanted.

Serves 4

Nutritional Analysis:
Calories: 65 • Protein: (g) 7 • Carbs: (g) 12 • Fat: (g) 1 •
Sat. Fat: (g) 0 • Cholesterol: (mg) 0 • Fiber: (g) 7 • Sodium: (mg) 60

Stuffed Red Peppers

This takes only minutes to prepare. The "boats" can bake with any meal or be the star of a vegetarian meal.

3 red peppers, whole, cut into wedges

----

3 med. zucchini, fresh, quartered lengthwise, sliced 1/4" thick
1/2 cup oat bran, uncooked
1/3 cup parmesan cheese, fresh grated — or soy parmesan
3 tbsp. parsley, fresh, chopped
3 tbsp. water — prefer pure
1 tbsp. olive oil
1 clove garlic, fresh, minced
1/2 tsp. thyme, dried leaf
1/2 tsp. basil, dried leaf
1/4 tsp. red pepper, flakes
1/4 tsp. salt, sea — or to taste

Directions:

1. Slice peppers into "boats" along their natural indentations.
2. Mix remaining ingredients in a bowl. Pack mixture into boats.
3. Bake at 375 degrees for 15 to 25 minutes or until tender.

Notes:

This can be prepared the night or morning before. Allow more time to cook if removing from the refrigerator.

Ingredient Substitutions:

Whole grain bread crumbs can replace the oat bran.
Soy parmesan can replace all or part of the parmesan.

   Freezes well.

Serves 5

Nutritional Analysis:
Calories: 102 • Protein: (g) 7 • Carbs: (g) 13 • Fat: (g) 6 •
Sat. Fat: (g) 2 • Cholesterol: (mg) 4 • Fiber: (g) 4 • Sodium: (mg) 214

Sweet Carrots

A simple way to prepare carrots that is sure to please every child.

  1 lb. carrots, fresh, sliced or julienned
  1 tsp. basil, dried leaf — or fresh
  2 tbsp. maple syrup — or to taste

Directions:

1. Steam carrots until tender. The smaller the pieces, the faster they cook.
2. Sprinkle the basil and maple syrup over the carrots. Toss to evenly distribute.

Notes:

Ingredient Substitutions:

Replace broccoli or cauliflower for the carrots.

Replace maple syrup with honey.

This is a good side dish for a grilled or grain dish.

Serves 4

Nutritional Analysis:

Calories: 55 • Protein: (g) 1 • Carbs: (g) 13 • Fat: (g) 0 •
Sat. Fat: (g) 0 • Cholesterol: (mg) 0 • Fiber: (g) 4 • Sodium: (mg) 44

Golden Hashbrowns

A wonderful dish that young and old will enjoy.

2 large potatoes, with skin, grated

----

1 tbsp. canola oil
1 med. onion, fresh, chopped
1 clove garlic, fresh, minced
1 whole carrot, fresh, grated
1 tsp. Parsley Patch Dill seasoning — or garlic seasoning

Directions:

1. Soak grated potatoes in cold water.
2. Sauté onion and garlic in oil until translucent in large skillet.
3. Drain potatoes and pat dry. Mix with carrot and Parsley Patch Seasoning or garlic salt.
4. Add potato mixture to onions. Cook until brown. Flip and cook other side.

Notes:

Time Saver Tips:

Use baked potatoes and grate instead of fresh.

Use food processor to quickly chop and grate all veggies.

Serves 4

Nutritional Analysis:

Calories: 217 • Protein: (g) 4 • Carbs: (g) 43 • Fat: (g) 4 •
Sat. Fat: (g) 0 • Cholesterol: (mg) 0 • Fiber: (g) 2 • Sodium: (mg) 18

Tex–Mex Corn

A quick vegetable combination that mixes well with any Mexican dish.

1 10–oz. pkg. corn, yellow, frozen, steamed

1/4 cup green onions, minced
1 tsp. canola oil — or stock

---

4 tsp. red pepper, chopped
2 oz. green chili peppers, canned, diced
1/2 tsp. cumin, ground

Directions:

1. While corn steams, sauté onion in oil or stock.
2. Stir in pepper, chilies and cumin.

Notes:

Ingredient Substitution:

Replace chilies with salsa.

This is a good side dish for Mexican dishes or grains.

Serves 3

Nutritional Analysis:

Calories: 106 • Protein: (g) 3 • Carbs: (g) 22 • Fat: (g) 2 •
Sat. Fat: (g) 0 • Cholesterol: (mg) 0 • Fiber: (g) 3 • Sodium: (mg) 141

Zippy Bok Choy

Bok choy is a wonderful alternative to cabbage in this dish.

2 tsp. olive oil — or stock
1 cup green onions, chopped
1 clove garlic, fresh, minced
1/4 tsp. ginger, ground — or grated fresh ginger

---

1 whole carrot, fresh, sliced or chopped
6 cups bok choy (Chinese cabbage), fresh, chopped

1/2 cup vegetable stock (from recipe) — or from veggie cubes
1/2 tsp. tamari — or to taste

Directions:

1. Sauté garlic, green onion and ginger in oil or stock.
2. Stir in carrot and bok choy.
3. Add stock and tamari and sauté until the liquid reduces.
4. Sprinkle with canola seeds or caraway seeds when serving.

Notes:

Ingredient Substitution:

Regular cabbage can replace the bok choy.

Ingredient Preference:

Fresh ginger adds more zip than dried.

This is a good side dish to a grilled entree.

Serves 3

Nutritional Analysis:

Calories: 70 • Protein: (g) 3 • Carbs: (g) 9 • Fat: (g) 4 •
Sat. Fat: (g) 0 • Cholesterol: (mg) 0 • Fiber: (g) 3 • Sodium: (mg) 162

Notes:

Crunchy Granola

Our favorite granola. A basic granola to which you can add anything. Make several batches and store in the refrigerator.

3 cups oats
1/2 cup flour, barley — or whole wheat
1/3 cup sunflower seeds
1/3 cup sesame seeds, hulled
1/3 cup almonds, slivered
1/4 cup pecans
1/2 tsp. cinnamon, ground
1/4 tsp. nutmeg, ground
1/4 tsp. salt, sea — optional

1/4 cup maple syrup — or other liquid sweetener
1/4 cup canola oil — optional
1 tsp. vanilla extract

Directions:

1. Mix dry ingredients.
2. Mix liquid ingredients and stir into the dry ingredients.
3. Spread on lightly oiled cookie sheet. Bake at 275 degrees until done. Stir every 10 minutes. Watch so it doesn't burn.

Add dried fruits when granola has cooled.

 Freezes well.

Makes 5 to 6 cups of granola
Serves 10

Nutritional Analysis:

Calories: 347 • Protein: (g) 3 • Carbs: (g) 34 • Fat: (g) 19 •
Sat. Fat: (g) 2 • Cholesterol: (mg) 0 • Fiber: (g) 2 • Sodium: (mg) 62

Oat Crackers

Another great compliment to a soup or salad dinner.

1/2 cup pecans
1 3/4 cups oats
1/2 tsp. salt, sea
1 tsp. baking powder
1 tsp. canola oil

----

1 cup soy milk

Directions:

1. Place all dry ingredients in food processor. Process until blended.
2. While processor is running, pour in oil.
3. While processor is running, pour in enough milk to make a dough that holds its shape but is not too sticky.
4. Roll out on prepared cookie sheet. Cut into squares.
5. Bake at 300 degrees until lightly browned.

Notes:

Crackers become crisper when cooled.

Ingredient Option:

Nuts can be omitted.

 Freezes well.

Serves 8

Nutritional Analysis:

Calories: 196 • Protein: (g) 7 • Carbs: (g) 25 • Fat: (g) 8 •
Sat. Fat: (g) 1 • Cholesterol: (mg) 0 • Fiber: (g) 1 • Sodium: (mg) 211

Cornbread

Some of the best cornbread I have ever eaten and so very simple.

1 cup soy milk — or rice or almond
1/4 cup honey — or other sweetener
1 large egg — or egg replacer
2 tbsp. canola oil

----

1 1/2 cups cornmeal, whole–grain, yellow
1/2 cup flour, barley — or whole wheat
1 tbsp. baking powder
3/4 tsp. salt, sea

Directions:

1. Mix liquid ingredients.
2. Mix dry ingredients and add to liquid ingredients.
3. Pour into lightly oiled 9" pan. Bake at 350 degrees for about 30 minutes or until done.

 Freezes well.

Serves 9

Nutritional Analysis:

Calories: 148 • Protein: (g) 3 • Carbs: (g) 24 • Fat: (g) 5 •
Sat. Fat: (g) 1 • Cholesterol: (mg) 24 • Fiber: (g) 2 • Sodium: (mg) 374

Green Onion Biscuits

A great variation from traditional biscuits. Make them small for soups and salads. Make them large and use as a sandwich base.

1 cup barley flour — or whole wheat pastry flour
1 cup spelt flour — or whole wheat pastry flour
4 tsp. baking powder
1/4 tsp. salt
1/2 cup green onions, minced
1 tsp. dry dill weed

----

5 tsp. butter — or SUBSTITUTE

3/4 cup buttermilk — approximately

Directions:

1. Mix dry ingredients in a mixing bowl.
2. Cut butter into the dry mixture.
3. Add buttermilk until well combined.
4. Place on floured board and knead just a couple of times until smooth. Pat dough into 1" thickness, cut using a biscuit cutter or drop by large spoonfuls onto an oiled baking sheet.
5. Bake at 375 degrees for 15 minutes, or until done.

 Freezes well.

Makes 12 biscuits

Nutritional Analysis:
Calories: 59 • Protein: (g) 2 • Carbs: (g) 9 • Fat: (g) 2 •
Sat. Fat: (g) 1 • Cholesterol: (mg) 5 • Fiber: (g) 1 • Sodium: (mg) 228

Pizza Crust

This is a yeast pizza crust. Check out the Pizza Crust without yeast for a yeast–free version.

3/4 cup water, medium hot
2 cups flour, spelt — or kamut
1 3/4 tbsp. yeast, active dry — or SAF instant yeast
1/2 tsp. salt, sea
1 tbsp. olive oil

Directions:

Yeast Option:

Bosch Universal method (make 3 to 4 times the recipe)–
1. Pour water into bowl.
2. Add remaining ingredients, in order, adding only enough flour to clean the sides of bowl.

Conventional method–
1. Place yeast in bowl with a few drops of honey, let proof.
2. Mix dry ingredients and add to water. Mix until a stiff dough forms. Knead until smooth and elastic. Cover and let rise 1 hour.

3. Roll out either version. If using a pizza paddle, roll out on paddle covered with cornmeal. Prick crust with a fork many times. Lightly brush with olive oil.
4. Bake at 425 degrees on preheated pizza stone (or use a pizza pan) for 5 minutes.
5. Pizza can be completed at this point. Or crusts can be cooled and frozen for future use at this point.

Notes:

Ingredient Options:

Whole wheat flour could be used in place of the spelt or kamut.

1 to 3 tsp. of herb blends, such as basil, oregano or thyme, can be added to the dough.

 Freezes well. Partially bake crust.

Serves 4

Nutritional Analysis:

Calories: 249 • Protein: (g) 10 • Carbs: (g) 46 • Fat: (g) 5 •
Sat. Fat: (g) 1 • Cholesterol: (mg) 0 • Fiber: (g) 9 • Sodium: (mg) 298

Oat Pecan Muffins

A family favorite. It makes a great snack the next day.

1 cup barley flour — or whole wheat, spelt or quinoa
1/2 cup oatmeal, regular, uncooked
1 1/4 tsp. baking powder
1/2 tsp. baking soda
1/4 tsp. sea salt
1/2 tsp. cinnamon
1/4 tsp. nutmeg

1/2 cup skim milk — or MILK SUBSTITUTE
1/4 cup maple syrup
2 tbsp. canola oil
1 large egg — or EGG SUBSTITUTE
1 whole banana, mashed — or 1 ripe peach, diced
2–4 tbsp. chopped pecans

Directions:

1. Mix all dry ingredients together.
2. Mix all liquid ingredients with the banana. Combine with dry ingredients and stir in the nuts.
3. Pour into oiled or lined muffin tins.
4. Bake at 400 degrees for 15 minutes or until done.

Note:

This recipe doubles well.

  Freezes well.

Makes 12 muffins

Nutritional Analysis:

Calories: 83 • Protein: (g) 2 • Carbs: (g) 10 • Fat: (g) 4 •
Sat. Fat: (g) 0 • Cholesterol: (mg) 18 • Fiber: (g) 1 • Sodium: (mg) 164

Cinnamon Muffins

Makes great low–fat, tasty muffins in a flash.

Triple
3/4 c.
1 1/2 c.
3 c.

4 1/2 c.
4 1/2 tsp.
2 1/4 tsp
1 1/2 tsp.
3/4 tsp.
1 1/2 tsp.
1 1/2 c.
3/4 c.

1/4 cup canola oil
1/2 cup maple syrup — or other sweetener
1   cup applesauce, unsweetened

----

1 1/2 cups flour, spelt — or alternative
1 1/2 tsp. baking powder
3/4 tsp. cinnamon, ground
1/2 tsp. baking soda
1/4 tsp. nutmeg, ground
1/2 tsp. salt, sea
1/2 cup raisins, seedless, packed, sulfide–free
1/4 cup pecans — optional

1/2 c. chopped apples (Apple Cinnamon Muffins)
Bake 20-25 minutes

Directions:

1. Mix liquid ingredients.
2. Mix dry ingredients and add to liquid ingredients.
3. Fill oiled or lined muffin tins 2/3 full.
4. Bake at 375 degrees about 15 minutes or until done. (20 minutes)

Notes:

Time Saver Tip:

Make a double or triple batch and freeze the extras.

   Freezes well.

Makes 12 muffins

Nutritional Analysis:

Calories: 137 • Protein: (g) 2 • Carbs: (g) 19 • Fat: (g) 6 •
Sat. Fat: (g) 1 • Cholesterol: (mg) 0 • Fiber: (g) 3 • Sodium: (mg) 212

Strawberry Scones

Similar to a biscuit, scones are a wonderful treat with a cup of herb tea or with a salad dinner.

1 1/4 cups strawberry granola
1 1/4 cup barley flour — or whole wheat pastry flour
1/4 cup granular sweetener
2 tsp. baking powder
1 tsp. cream of tartar

----

3 tbsp. butter — or SUBSTITUTE

----

1 egg white — or EGG SUBSTITUTE
1/2 cup yogurt

1/2 cup strawberries, diced

Directions:

1. Place granola in blender and blend until crumbly. Use 1 cup of the granola and add all dry ingredients.
2. Cut in butter until crumbly.
3. Mix liquid ingredients and add to dry ingredients.
4. Gently stir in strawberries.
5. Pat dough into a 10" circle onto greased baking sheet, add flour if necessary. Cut into 12 wedges with a floured knife.
6. Bake at 375 degrees for 20 minutes, or until done.

Makes 12 scones

Nutritional Analysis:

Calories: 112 • Protein: (g) 2 • Carbs: (g) 12 • Fat: (g) 6 •
Sat. Fat: (g) 2 • Cholesterol: (mg) 8 • Fiber: (g) 1 • Sodium: (mg) 94

Notes:

Apple Muffins

2 egg whites
3/4 c. milk (soy, rice, almond)
1 medium apple, grated or chopped
1/2 c. currants
1/4 c. canola oil
1/3 c. honey — or maple syrup
1 3/4 c. spelt flour — or whole wheat
1 TBSP. baking powder
1/2 tsp. cinnamon

1. Beat egg whites and stir in milk, apple, currants, oil and honey.
2. Mix together dry ingredients.
3. Combine and stir briefly.
4. Fill oiled or lined muffin tin 2/3 - 3/4 full.
5. Bake 400° 15-20 minutes.

Peanut Butter Bread (Muffins)

1/2 c. almond butter
1/2 c. honey — or other sweetener
3 TBSP. oil
2 eggs
1/2 c. carrot, grated
2 medium ripe bananas, mashed
1/4 c. milk (soy, rice, almond)
1/4 tsp. cinnamon and nutmeg and allspice
1 tsp. vanilla
1/8 tsp. salt
1 tsp. baking powder
1 tsp. baking soda
1 3/4 c. spelt flour — or whole wheat

1. Blend almond butter, honey, oil, eggs, carrots, and bananas. Add the milk.
2. Mix dry ingredients and add to almond butter mixture.
3. Bake 300°. 3 oiled mini loaf pans about 30 minutes.
4. Can be made in muffin pans.

French Dressing

This is a dressing to substitute for commercial dressings that have dairy and sugar.

- 1/2 cup carrot juice, canned — prefer fresh
- 1/2 cup soy milk — or rice or almond milk
- 1/4 cup canola oil
- 1/4 cup tahini — or to taste
- 1 tbsp. mustard, stone ground
- 1 tbsp. vinegar, cider
- 1/4 tsp. salt, sea — or to taste

Directions:

Blend all ingredients in blender.

Makes about 1 3/4 cups dressing
Serves 25

Nutritional Analysis:

Calories: 38 • Protein: (g) 1 • Carbs: (g) 1 • Fat: (g) 4 •
Sat. Fat: (g) 0 • Cholesterol: (mg) 0 • Fiber: (g) 0 • Sodium: (mg) 36

Green Goddess Dressing

This is a dressing to substitute for commercial dressings that have dairy ingredients.

1   cup soy milk — or rice or almond milk
1/4 cup canola oil — or juice
2   tsp. vinegar, umeboshi — or cider, to taste
2   tbsp. tahini — or to taste
1   whole green onion, chopped
1   clove garlic, fresh, chopped
2   tbsp. parsley, Italian, fresh, chopped
1/4 tsp. salt, sea — or to taste

Directions:

Mix all ingredients in blender and blend until smooth.

Makes about 1 3/4 cups of dressing
Serves 25

Nutritional Analysis:

Calories: 30 • Protein: (g) 1 • Carbs: (g) 1 • Fat: (g) 3 •
Sat. Fat: (g) 0 • Cholesterol: (mg) 0 • Fiber: (g) 0 • Sodium: (mg) 26

Poppy Seed Dressing

A delightful dressing on a spinach or any mixed green salad.

1/3 cup honey
1/3 cup canola oil — or apple juice
2 tbsp. sesame seeds, hulled
1 tbsp. poppy seeds — optional
1/4 cup vinegar, cider — or flavored

Directions:

1. Place all ingredients in jar and screw lid on top.
2. Shake until well blended.

Makes about 1 cup of dressing
Serves 16

Nutritional Analysis:

Calories: 71 • Protein: (g) 0 • Carbs: (g) 6 • Fat: (g) 5 •
Sat. Fat: (g) 0 • Cholesterol: (mg) 0 • Fiber: (g) 0 • Sodium: (mg) 1

Mushroom Sauce

A superb sauce that is a favorite. Use it on mashed potatoes, grain dishes or veggies.

1/2 med. onion, fresh, minced
3/4 lb. mushrooms, fresh, thick sliced
1 1/2 tbsp. canola oil — or stock

1/4 cup rice flour, brown

---

2 tsp. tamari — or to taste
2 cups soy milk — or stock

Directions:

1. Sauté onions and mushrooms in oil or stock.
2. Stir in rice flour to form a roux.
3. Using a whisk or fork, slowly add milk to form a smooth sauce. Stir in tamari. Cook until thickened.

 Freezes well.

Makes about 3 cups of sauce
Serves 6

Nutritional Analysis:

Calories: 459 • Protein: (g) 11 • Carbs: (g) 85 • Fat: (g) 8 •
Sat. Fat: (g) 1 • Cholesterol: (mg) 0 • Fiber: (g) 7 • Sodium: (mg) 132

Tahini Dip

A mayonnaise substitute to use as a spread.

1   cup tahini
1/2   cup water
1/4   cup yogurt
1/4   cup lemon juice
2   cloves garlic, minced
1/2   tsp. Vege Sal

Directions:

Blend all ingredients in blender until smooth.

Notes:

Ingredient Substitution:

Firm tofu can be used in place of the yogurt. Replace yogurt with 1/4 cup tofu and 2 tbsp. oil.

Makes about 2 cups of spread

Nutritional Analysis:

Calories: 86 • Protein: (g) 3 • Carbs: (g) 3 • Fat: (g) 8 •
Sat. Fat: (g) 1 • Cholesterol: (mg) 0 • Fiber: (g) 1 • Sodium: (mg) 142

Miso Tahini Dip

A great dip.

> 3 tbsp. tahini
> 3 tbsp. white miso
> 2 tbsp. lemon juice — or to taste
> 1/4 cup water

Directions:

Blend all in blender until smooth.

Makes 3/4 cup dip

Nutritional Analysis:

Calories: 90 • Protein: (g) 3 • Carbs: (g) 3 • Fat: (g) 8 •
Sat. Fat: (g) 1 • Cholesterol: (mg) 0 • Fiber: (g) 1 • Sodium: (mg) 300

Honey Butter

A simple combination with many uses.

2 tbsp. butter, unsalted
2 tbsp. canola oil
1/3 cup honey

Directions:

Mix together and whip until creamy. Store in refrigerator.

Serves 4

Nutritional Analysis:

Calories: 198 • Protein: (g) 0 • Carbs: (g) 23 • Fat: (g) 13 •
Sat. Fat: (g) 4 • Cholesterol: (mg) 15 • Fiber: (g) 0 • Sodium: (mg) 2

Berry Good Syrup

This presents unlimited opportunities for variations.

    1/4 cup dates, chopped
    1 cup strawberries, fresh
    2 tbsp. honey — to taste

Directions:

1. Mix all in food processor or blender until smooth.
2. Serve warm over pancakes or at room temperature with muffins.

Note:

Ingredient Variation:

Substitute blueberries or raspberries for the strawberries.

Serves 6

Nutritional Analysis:

Calories: 49 • Protein: (g) 0 • Carbs: (g) 13 • Fat: (g) 0 •
Sat. Fat: (g) 0 • Cholesterol: (mg) 0 • Fiber: (g) 1 • Sodium: (mg) 1

Almond Crunch Bars

A great variation of the old time Rice Krispies Treats. My family says these taste better.

1/2 cup honey — prefer rice syrup
1/2 cup almond butter, plain
1/4 cup peanut butter, smooth, no salt — fresh or almond
2 tsp. vanilla extract

1/4 cup almonds, slivered
1/2 cup chocolate chips, semi–sweet — Sunspire brand
3 cups cereal, crispy rice
1/2 1.3–oz. box cereal, Grape Nuts — or Perky's Nutty Rice

Directions:

1. Combine sweetener and butters. Heat on low until melted. Stir in vanilla. Remove from heat.
2. Mix cereal, nuts and chips.
3. Stir in nut butter mixture. Pack tightly into lightly oiled 9" x 13" pan. Let cool about 10 minutes. Cut into squares.
4. Refrigerate, covered.

 Freezes well.

Makes 36 cookies

Nutritional Analysis:

Calories: 77 • Protein: (g) 2 • Carbs: (g) 9 • Fat: (g) 4 •
Sat. Fat: (g) 1 • Cholesterol: (mg) 0 • Fiber: (g) 0 • Sodium: (mg) 22

Blueberry Cheesecake Bars

A recipe even "tofu–haters" will enjoy.

2/3 cup maple syrup
3 cups flour, spelt — or whole wheat
1/4 cup water

---

2 pkg. Mori Nu "lite" tofu, firm
2/3 cup honey
2 tsp. vanilla extract
1 3/4 large egg whites — or egg substitute
2 tbsp. flour, spelt — or whole wheat

---

3 cups blueberries — or more

Directions:

1. Mix water, syrup and flour with fork or in food processor until crumbly.
2. Place half of crumbs in lightly oiled 9" x 13" pan.
3. Blend tofu, honey, vanilla, egg whites and flour in blender until smooth. Pour over crust.
4. Sprinkle blueberries over filling. Sprinkle with remaining crumbs. Bake at 350 degrees for about 40 minutes or until middle is firm. Cool before cutting.

  Freezes well.

Serves 12

Nutritional Analysis:

Calories: 206 • Protein: (g) 8 • Carbs: (g) 44 • Fat: (g) 1 •
Sat. Fat: (g) 0 • Cholesterol: (mg) 0 • Fiber: (g) 17 • Sodium: (mg) 48

Rich Bars

A favorite that dispels the myth that tofu can't taste almost decadent.

1/3 cup pecans, minced
1/4 tsp. salt, sea
2 1/2 cups flour, barley — or whole wheat pastry
1 tbsp. canola oil
1/2 cup water — or more

---

1 pkg. Mori Nu "lite" tofu, firm
3/4 cup maple syrup — more if want sweet
1/4 cup flour, barley — or whole wheat
1 tsp. vanilla extract
1/2 tsp. baking powder

1/2 cup pecans — minced
2/3 cup dates, chopped
2/3 cup chocolate chips, semi–sweet (Sunspire brand)

Directions:

1. Mix dry ingredients. Stir in oil and water until crumbly. Pack into lightly oiled 9" x 13" pan.
2. Blend tofu, syrup, vanilla, flour and baking powder in blender until smooth.
3. Stir nuts, dates and chips into tofu mixture by hand. Pour over crust. Bake at 425 degrees for 15 minutes, then 350 degrees for 15 to 20 minutes. Chill. Store in refrigerator.

  Freezes well.

Serves 36

Nutritional Analysis:
Calories: 48 • Protein: (g) 1 • Carbs: (g) 5 • Fat: (g) 3 •
Sat. Fat: (g) 1 • Cholesterol: (mg) 1 • Fiber: (g) 3 • Sodium: (mg) 29

Meals in 30 Minutes

Fudgy Brownies

A gooey brownie, low in fat.

3/4 cup whole wheat pastry flour
1/2 cup barley flour — or whole wheat pastry flour
2 tbsp. arrowroot powder
3/4 cup cocoa powder
1/4 cup Sucanat, FruitSource or DevanSweet
1 1/2 tsp. baking powder
1/2 tsp. sea salt
1/2 tsp. cinnamon

1/3 pkg. Mori Nu "lite" tofu, firm
1/2 cup Just Like Shortenin'*
1 cup maple syrup
1 1/2 tsp. vanilla

1/3 cup Sunspire chocolate chips — optional

Directions:

1. Mix dry ingredients in bowl.
2. Mix tofu, JLS, syrup and vanilla in blender until smooth.
3. Combine tofu mixture with dry ingredients. Stir in chips.
4. Bake in lightly oiled 7" x 11" baking dish at 350 degrees for 25 to 30 minutes or until done.

Note:

* Made with apples, plums and water, JLS is an excellent egg and fat substitute. Call 800-301-6580 for retailer nearest you.

 Freezes well.

Serves 12

Nutritional Analysis:

Calories: 175 • Protein: (g) 3 • Carbs: (g) 40 • Fat: (g) 2 •
Sat. Fat: (g) 1 • Cholesterol: (mg) 1 • Fiber: (g) 5 • Sodium: (mg) 168

Carrot Mini Cakes

A tasty quick bread that comes together quickly.

2 1/2 cups barley flour — or whole wheat flour
1 cup oats
1 1/2 tsp. baking soda
1 tsp. baking powder
1 tsp. cinnamon
1 tbsp. arrowroot

---

1 1/2 cup sweetener — honey
1/4 cup oil
1/2 cup milk — or orange juice or water

1/2 cup applesauce
1 cup raisins
2 cups grated carrots
3 egg whites

Directions:

1. Combine dry ingredients.
2. Beat egg whites until frothy.
3. Beat honey and oil in another bowl. Add water to honey.
4. Add flour mixture to honey mixture. Fold in raisins, nuts, and carrots. Fold in egg whites.
5. Place in oiled mini–loaf pans or oiled or lined muffin tins and bake at 350 degrees for 20 minutes or until done.

 Freezes well.

Makes 3 mini loaves or 12 muffins

Nutritional Analysis:

Calories: 279 • Protein: (g) 4 • Carbs: (g) 59 • Fat: (g) 6 •
Sat. Fat: (g) 1 • Cholesterol: (mg) 0 • Fiber: (g) 1 • Sodium: (mg) 228

Apple Cherry Crisp

A delicious dessert. Not the best food combining.

4   whole apples, fresh, sliced
2   cups cherries, fresh, sour, pitted — or 1 can
2   tbsp. arrowroot powder — or cornstarch
1   tsp. vanilla extract

3/4   cup rice flour, brown — or whole wheat
3/4   cup Perky's Nutty Rice cereal — or Grape Nuts
1/4   cup honey — or granular sweetener
2   tbsp. canola oil

Directions:

1. Mix apples, cherries, arrowroot and vanilla together. Place in prepared deep baking dish.
2. Mix dry ingredients together. Stir together honey (heated) and oil. Mix with dry ingredients. Add enough water to make crumbly. (Can be done in food processor.)
3. Crumble over fruit. Bake at 325 degrees for about 25 minutes or until done.

Note:

Ingredient Option:

1/4 – 1/2 cup sweetener can be added to fruit: cook until soft and then proceed.

 Freezes well.

Serves 8

Nutritional Analysis:

Calories: 186 • Protein: (g) 2 • Carbs: (g) 37 • Fat: (g) 4 •
Sat. Fat: (g) 0 • Cholesterol: (mg) 0 • Fiber: (g) 3 • Sodium: (mg) 3

Apple Pie

An easy pie with infinite variations.

   2   9" pie crusts, frozen

----

12 – 8   whole apples, fresh, sliced

if store bought   1/2   cup honey — or granular sweetener

   1/4   cup arrowroot powder — 1/3 cup

   2   tsp. lemon juice, fresh

   1/4   tsp. cinnamon, ground

   1/4   tsp. nutmeg, ground

   1/4   cup raisins, seedless, unpacked

Directions:

1. Place one crust in bottom of pie pan.
2. Mix apples with remaining ingredients and place on top of crust.
3. Cover with second crust. Flute edges. Bake at 450 degrees for 15 minutes, then 30 minutes at 350 degrees or until done.

 Freezes well.

Serves 8

Nutritional Analysis:

Calories: 336 • Protein: (g) 2 • Carbs: (g) 61 • Fat: (g) 11 •
Sat. Fat: (g) 3 • Cholesterol: (mg) 1 • Fiber: (g) 4 • Sodium: (mg) 207

Notes:

PART II:

Creative Cooking

"Creative" Cooking

I can't tell you how many times I have tried to be "organized" and prepared a month's worth of food in one day! I have read the books, tried recipes and suffered exhaustion after trying each "easy" new program. The thought of ever cooking again after one of those marathons was totally repulsive. Sound familiar? This scene doesn't even address the fact that these "once–a–month" recipes were far from healthy. Is there any hope for those of us who want healthy food available, without cooking every day or buying expensive, tasteless convenient health food? YES!

As usual, to solve a problem, I find it helpful to isolate the issues and then find a simple approach to address those issues. So, let's take a look at the needs and reasons for "creative" cooking.

⊕ Less time in the kitchen
Most of us want great meals with minimal preparation time. We want a "wife" to magically appear and prepare, serve and clean up after a delicious, nutritious meal. Doesn't that sound wonderful?

⊕ Convenient food that is also healthy and tasty
Most people think health food requires more cooking time — doesn't cooking from scratch require being home and cooking at least four hours every day? Or, they think it must taste terrible and look worse. The alternative often

seems to be our old standby, easy–to–make recipes that ignore health considerations. Is it possible to marry convenience with health and taste?

⏱ Cut costs and trim the monthly food budget
The most common concern in eating healthy food is cost. So often traditional bulk cooking depends on canned soups, white pasta, sugar, nitrate–loaded meats and chemically–laden foods. How can we eliminate these ingredients, stay within a budget and yet do bulk cooking?

Time, convenience, money — they drive us away from bulk cooking, yet also pull us toward convenience foods. The tension can cause an overwhelming sense of hopelessness.

OK, now we know the issues. So, where is that "simple" solution? Just as we addressed meal planning, in *Food Smart!* and *Lifestyle for Health*, with a different approach, so we will address once–a–month cooking with a different approach. With meal planning, we didn't plan 21 meals per week or 130 meals a month. Instead, we looked at seven cooking methods for different days of the week. Using seasonal foods and these methods (breakfast and lunch were addressed separately), we simplified a 130–meal monster with a 7–fisted punch. The meal–planning monster was tamed.

Let's do the same thing with the once–a–month cooking marathon. Let's dissolve the marathon into several quick sprints. Rather than a marathon cooking day that requires 29 days from which to recover, our goal is to minimize time spent in the kitchen, provide healthy, tasty food conveniently, and spend less money.

To sprint means to run at full speed for a short distance. The following six sprints can be combined in a multitude of ways. Each combination will take you and your family to new vistas. Your speed can range from walking to running. The distance can be a set course or just a walk around the block. The variety is endless, the scenery is seasonal, the finish line is a treat as you once again sit down to a tasty, healthy, convenient meal in record time.

I will give an overview of each of these sprints in this chapter. The next six chapters will go into each sprint in more detail and give practical examples, recipes and methods.

Let's set that marathon aside and begin our tour. What fun ... I think I see hope dawning across the checkered horizon.

First Sprint — Beat the Clock with Bulk Cooking
Have you ever noticed that when you have a job to do such as paint or wallpaper, the hardest parts seem to be in the set–up time and the clean–up time? The actual painting, wallpapering, etc. seems to go quickly.

The same principle works with cooking. The preparation and clean–up time seem to be the hardest. Bulk cooking allows you to minimize the prep and clean–up time. How? Making four dozen muffins takes almost the same time to set up and clean up as making one dozen. However, you have four times the food for the same time investment.

In the bulk–cooking chapter, we will look at foods that easily lend themselves to cooking in bulk. You will also find recipes, tips and recommendations to make this sprint enjoyable and one of the easiest.

② Second Sprint — Face–lift the Leftovers

The average American family complains at the sight of leftovers. The thought of the same food three days in a row is beyond comprehension. The alternative is a face–lift. Recently I took cooked black beans and steamed broccoli through the following face–lift:

Meal one: Black bean enchiladas with steamed broccoli

Meal two: Cold summer salad with black beans, broccoli, cherry tomatoes and feta cheese over mixed greens with cornbread

Meal three: Vegetarian pizza with broccoli and other toppings

Meal four: Black bean soup and cornbread

Does that look like leftovers to you? The leftovers were the individual ingredients, not the actual recipe. In the chapter on leftovers, we will learn to distinguish between ingredients that can be used in many ways and eating the same recipe over and over. You will find many basic ingredients with numerous face lift possibilities. A tuck here and a tweak there will present simple food in a dashing new way to your family.

③ Sprint Three — Use the Freezer and Multiply

A freezer is almost a requirement for having extra food on hand. Other food preservation methods, such as canning and dehydrating, are also available. Canning removes more nutrients than the other two methods. I also find it the least enjoyable, so we will focus on freezing and a little on dehydrating.

Knowing how to use a freezer, and which one to buy, can make a freezer a very cost effective appliance to have available. The chapter on the freezer will provide tips on what foods freeze well, how to freeze and what to do with frozen foods.

Sprint Four — Share the Fun With Friends

Having a friend join you in your sprint can make the experience much more enjoyable. Having a friendly chat with your best friend may seem out of reach in your busy schedule. However, if that chat happens while you are bulk cooking dozens of muffins, well, you seem to have hit two birds with one stone.

There are so many ways to include a friend(s) in this creative cooking process. In the sharing–the–fun–with–a–friend chapter, you will find many ways to let your social side enjoy the work process. You will also learn how to set up a co–op, buy in bulk and store that food so it doesn't spoil.

Sprint Five — Nurture "Heart" Healthy Cooking Skills

A genius is often the person that can go beyond the perceived lines of a square and see the roundness of a circle. Cooking is not just legally following black words on a white page. Cooking can be the expression of creativity that takes the basics, infuses it with love and produces real nourishment.

In this simple chapter, I will share some of our favorite combinations. You will also have an opportunity to learn how to cook for fun, not just because you have to put a meal on the table. Learn to nurture others and you will be nourished yourself.

Beat the Clock with Bulk Cooking

For many people cooking a month of food in one day doesn't work. This approach is also more difficult when you want 50% of your food to be produce (fresh, when possible). However, bulk cooking (cooking for more than one meal at a time) does multiply savings. When you cook in bulk, you can experience savings in the following areas:

🕐 Saves time spent in the kitchen and at the grocery store

🕐 Saves money spent on impulse buying

🕐 Saves money spent eating out (food is available at home)

🕐 Saves energy — personal, electrical and automotive — and decreases food waste

As you begin to consider bulk cooking, be sure you know your eating patterns. You may want to revise those patterns as you learn more about healthy eating. Cooking in bulk will allow you the freedom to plan meals that are good for you, as well as easy on your schedule and budget.

I have found that shopping on a monthly budget (with weekly produce runs to the store) is a big savings of time, energy and money. I also have food on hand to handle the continual stream of guests that meander through our home. We love to have friends in for a meal and fellowship. Having food on hand makes that gift flow much more easily.

The Pantry

To shop once a month, you must prepare a pantry list. I keep a running list (it's a mental list at this point) of all pantry basics. Based on what I have used the previous month, I add that plus any expected hospitality activities or bulk cooking needs to my monthly grocery list.

If you are a beginner to bulk cooking, use the following suggested pantry list as a place to start. Adjust it to meet your needs. You might want to keep a copy taped to your pantry, in a handy file or on your cupboard door. As you run out of an item, make a check next to it. The checked items become the basis of your grocery list (whether a weekly, bi–weekly or monthly list). Since the list is by categories, it will also come closer to reflecting a store layout and expedite your shopping time.

Our *Lifestyle for Health* cookbook has an expanded glossary of any food you might find unfamiliar. We have added the more familiar alternative to help you understand the foods we use. Choosing to start with the more familiar food is acceptable. Learning to eat healthy is a process. In Appendix C you will find a list of preferred brands. This is a list of products our family finds to be consistently tasty and affordable.

Pantry List:

Baking Supplies
almond extract
arrowroot powder (cornstarch)
baking powder (aluminum–free)
biscuit mixes (whole grain)
carob powder (cocoa powder)

dried fruit
flour (whole grain)
oils (expeller pressed)
vanilla
yeast

Beverages
herbal teas
juice (organic, sugar–free)
lemonade (organic, sugar–free)
spritzers (sugar–free, all juice)

Canned and/or Packaged
beans
broth (chicken or veggie)
chilies
chips (low–fat)
crackers (whole grain)
pasta (whole grain)
pasta sauce
refried beans
salsa
soups (no msg)
tofu (Mori Nu brand)
tomatoes (Muir brand)

Condiments
catsup
jams (fruit only)
mayonnaise
miso
mustard
salad dressings
tahini

tamari (soy sauce)
vinegar (cider or flavored – no white)
Worcestershire sauce

Grains
barley
brown rice (regular and quick cooking)
cereals
crackers (whole grain)
granola
millet
oat bran
oatmeal
quinoa

Nuts, Seeds and Snacks
almonds
cashews
pecans
popcorn
pretzels
pumpkin seeds
sesame seeds
sunflower seeds
walnuts

Refrigerator and/or Frozen Foods
butter (I don't recommend margarine)
cheese (dairy, soy, rice or almond)
eggs (free–range, fertile)
fruit (prefer fresh or frozen to canned)
meat (seitan, vegetarian options)
milk (dairy, soy, rice or almond)
tofu

tortillas (whole grain)
vegetables (prefer fresh or frozen to canned)

Spices and Herbs

allspice	basil
bay leaves	cardamon
cayenne	celery seeds
chervil	chili powder
chives	cinnamon
cloves	cumin
curry powder	dillweed
dry mustard	fennel seeds
garlic powder	ginger
marjoram	minced garlic
minced onion	nutmeg
oregano	parsley
pepper	poultry seasoning
red pepper flakes	rosemary
sage	sea salt
tarragon	thyme

Sweeteners

brown rice syrup
FruitSource (a brand)
maple syrup
molasses
raw, unfiltered honey
Sucanat (a brand)

Planning

The key to creative, bulk cooking is to have a plan and to work the plan. The plan can be broken into four key areas.

    1. Recipe selection
    2. Shopping and container selection

3. Quantity cooking, packaging and labeling
4. Clean–up and celebration

Recipe Selection

When selecting the recipes, consider the season, family likes and dislikes, time available and prices. For example, during the end of summer, many produce items are available at very low prices. Taking advantage of squash, tomatoes, peppers, and other bargains could easily lead to bulk cooking of lasagna, salsa, moussaka or other casseroles or pasta sauces. During the fall, when pumpkin and winter squash is on sale, pumpkin bread, cooked pumpkin (frozen) and squash soups could be cooked easily and inexpensively.

While selecting recipes, consider store sales, farmer's market produce (summer low prices) and other food pricing options. Many times larger containers of special foods are available at significant savings. Don't, however, substitute quality for a lower price. Our goal is healthy, tasty food, not simply quantity.

Be sure to prepare foods your family likes when you bulk cook. Nothing is more frustrating than preparing five batches of a recipe, only to find your family hates the dish. Check the recipe in a single batch with your family.

Another key in recipe selection is to select recipes that have compatible preparation activities. For example, while making several batches of lasagna, have potatoes baking for Twice Baked Potatoes. When the lasagna is finished, finish the potatoes. These two recipes dovetail together easily. Usually two to four recipes per cooking "sprint" works best. Do more of fewer recipes to keep the work load simplified. If you only have a couple of hours, then pick only one or two recipes.

Meals in 30 Minutes

Once you determine your regular pantry list, it is time to select the food that you will cook in bulk. You may decide on a day of baking, pasta (making homemade pasta), soups, casseroles, desserts, side dishes, etc. Or, you might decide to make a multiple of each meal for one week (i.e., make two or three batches of each meal for the following week). Either way, you will be making extra food for another day.

Whatever your approach, it's time to select recipes. Combine some of your favorites with some of the new ones in this book or another book. Make sure they are simple enough not to present a problem when multiplied. Our *Lifestyle for Health* cookbook helps you customize your own recipes to make them healthier. Bulk food only expedites disease and sickness if it's not healthy.

Be sure to check out our eight weekly menus and computerized menu planning software. It is discussed fully in our *Lifestyle for Health* cookbook. Having a computerized program (we recommend Dinner!) can help you quickly select recipes, see a week's nutritional analysis and produce a weekly grocery list with approximate cost for the groceries, all at the touch of a button. This makes planning so much easier. Since you can also use your own favorite recipes, you can start with food with which you are familiar.

In this book you will find notations after each recipe as to whether the recipe freezes well. The following section lists some of our favorite family recipes that freeze well from two of our other cookbooks. Pick a few and add some of your favorites and you can sprint ahead of the best restaurant in town.

Lifestyle for Health **(LFH) cookbook**
Soups:
Black Bean Soup
Borscht
Brunswick Stew
Cream of "Chicken" Soup
Curried Lentil Soup
Gazpacho
Gumbo
Lentil Soup
Minestrone

Sauces:
Eggplant Pasta Sauce
Enchilada Sauce
Homemade Tomato Sauce

Vegetables:
Peachy Carrots
Refried Beans
Stuffed Squash

Breads:
Buckwheat Mini Loaves
Crunchy Granola
Oatmeal Muffins
Oatmeal Pancakes
Pancakes or Waffles
Pumpkin Muffins
Rice Flour Banana Bread

Main Dishes:
Baked Beans
Chili

Chili Rellenos Casserole
Egg Rolls (freeze before cooking)
Lentil Loaf
Low–Fat Lasagna
Moussaka
Red Beans and Rice
Squash Boats (Only partially bake)
Vegetable Deep Dish Pie

Desserts:
Apple Cake
Black Forest Cake (freeze components separate, assemble when thawed)
Carob Raisin Chews
Gingerbread
Oat'n Honey Cake
Oatrageous Cookies
Peanut Butter Blossoms
Pop in Pan Freezer Peach Pie or Crisp
Raspberry Bars
Space Balls
Tollhouse Cookies
Wintry Pumpkin Sheet Cake
Yeah! for Brownies

Kid's Favorites **cookbook:**
Apple Muffins
Burrito Cups
Carob or Chocolate Syrup
Kid's Zucchini Lasagna
Oatmeal Chocolate Chip Cake
Pancake and Biscuit Mix
Peanut Butter Bread

Sesame "Chicken" (make with extra sauce)
Waffles (blueberry or nut)
Yellow Enchiladas (freeze components separately)

Shopping, Appliance and Container Selection

Plan to shop the day before you cook. Getting the food
(whether in a store or a co–op), washing the produce,
organizing appliances and getting all of the containers ready
can take several hours. Begin cooking the next day.
Spreading out the work makes it seem like less work. With
two people, another option is for person one to do the
shopping, both do the cooking and person two to clean up.

To expedite shopping, write every ingredient on
your list by category (i.e., produce, grocery, freezer, dairy,
meat, etc.). Check to be sure you have all of the basics in
the recipe (i.e., flour, oil, herbs, etc.). It's very frustrating
to be in the middle of cooking and find you have only half
of the needed spice, herb or baking powder.

Double check your multiplication of all ingredients.
If each person wants four times the recipe and there are two
people cooking, you actually need to make eight times the
recipe. If a recipe calls for one 8 oz. can of tomato sauce,
and you are making eight times the recipe, see if larger
containers are available than just 8 oz. cans. Be sure to
multiply out each ingredient. This is a step so often
overlooked by the first–time bulk cook.

Stick to your list when you shop. The goal of saving
money is quickly lost if you yield to every temptation a
grocery store offers. To prevent that weakness, simply don't
pick up a tempting product. You can't buy it if you never
pick it up and put it in the cart.

On shopping day, put groceries away and wash
produce. All produce should be washed, even organic, to

extend its life and to increase taste. We use a wash of a few drops of Shaklee's Basic H in a sink of water for all of our produce (except mushrooms and onions). You could also use Clorox, lemon juice and other products by Amway, Melaluka or NeoLife.

It is helpful to set out the appliances you will use for your bulk cooking. A blender, food processor or salad shooter is invaluable. If you don't have these items, borrow them on your bulk cooking day. Pasta machines make pasta in a matter of minutes (whole grain pasta is just as easy as white flour pasta). A tortilla maker makes homemade tortillas quick and easy. A pressure cooker cooks beans and legumes in mere minutes. Champion juicers easily make applesauce, refried beans and other foods of this texture.

Spend some time thinking through the equipment that will save you time on your bulk cooking day. Try to borrow any equipment you don't have. A Bosch Universal kitchen machine will allow you to make six pounds of homemade bread dough in just eight minutes. You can then use this dough for bread, pizza, sandwiches, pecan rolls or other delights. (The *Lifestyle for Health* cookbook contains an expanded list of other helpful appliances.) Contact our office for equipment information. Over time, an investment in the right equipment will save you hours in the kitchen.

Container selection varies, based on the type of recipe. I have found that zip–lock type freezer bags work well. They are lightweight, reusable and come in several sizes. Select the size of container based on the number of desired servings per use.

If you choose to use glass baking dishes, line the pan with aluminum foil and another layer of wax paper. (Parchment paper can also substitute for these other papers.)

Allow extra paper to completely wrap the entire dish. Place the lasagna, casserole, pie, etc. into the lined dish. Freeze. When frozen, finish wrapping the casserole in more foil/wax paper (or parchment). Remove from the pan, label and freeze.

Muffins and small breads fit well into gallon sized bags. Soups and liquid–based dishes can go into pint, quart or gallon sized bags depending on serving sizes. Small pizza shells fit into gallon or bread bags.

Quantity Cooking, Packaging and Labeling

Now the fun begins. You have all of the food, the produce is washed and the containers are ready. The next step is to set out all necessary cooking utensils, measuring cups and small appliances.

Think through each recipe. To save time, perform all similar tasks at one time. For example, do all shredding or slicing, etc. at one time. Once all similar tasks are complete, do all other prep work. While a sauce is cooking, something else can be baking. Take advantage of all burners, ovens and crockpots.

Now it's time to assemble the various recipes, if you are doing main dishes. When assembling, separate according to your family's needs. If you are making six batches of soup, separate out the appropriate quantity for you or your family's needs and place in a container.

When packed, set the food aside to cool. You do not want to place a lot of hot food directly into the freezer. This will begin to thaw other foods and slow the freezing of the new food. Add food to the freezer in batches. As one batch freezes, add the next batch. Or, cool in refrigerator and then add to the freezer. If it is cold outside, set covered food outside to cool and then freeze.

Be sure to label the contents. It is so easy to forget what is in that small bag at the back of the freezer. The label should contain the name of recipe, date, quantity and any reheating or assembly instructions (or refer to cookbook and page number).

To complete this process, it is helpful to prepare a list of dishes being added to the freezer. Keeping an ongoing list of freezer contents can ensure efficient use of all frozen foods. You don't want that hard work to wind up in a trash can because it sat in the freezer too long.

Cleanup and Celebration

To help with cleanup, I recommend having two sets of measuring cups and spoons. Use one for wet and one for dry ingredients. This virtually eliminates cleaning between measuring assignments.

Other Time–saving Tips

🕐 Sauté several items in a skillet in quick succession. Rinsing between dishes is rarely necessary.

🕐 Undercook dishes with grains or pasta to prevent a mushy finished product.

🕐 An electric skillet can serve as an extra burner.

🕐 Reuse mixing bowls. Many times a bowl needs no rinsing or a quick rinse to be ready for the next task.

If you keep the work areas somewhat orderly as you cook, cleanup should take only about 30 minutes. Cleanup can begin while food is cooking or cooling.

Once cleanup is complete, be sure to take some time to rest and celebrate. Have a cup of your favorite tea and a "treat." You have sprinted to the finish of this race, so enjoy yourself. If you just made muffins, enjoy a warm muffin with your tea. You've earned it, enjoy it!

Face–lift the Leftovers

Knowing how to use a basic ingredient(s) in many ways is the basis of creative leftovers. For instance, I never make just the amount of brown rice for one recipe, I always make extra for the remainder of the week.

As you read the list of various basic ingredients, and their many different uses, begin to think of your favorite foods. How could they be served? Could they be put in soups, salads, on pizza or in a tortilla? For further ideas, be sure to check out the meal planning methods described in the Meal Planning chapter in *Food Smart!* (1994 by Piñon Press).

The following ingredients can be easily used in many forms. Use this list as a springboard for many exciting meals. Be sure to check the index of all of our *Lifestyle for Health* cookbooks. Main ingredients are listed with all recipes using that ingredient. If you have extra of any one ingredient, this topical list will give you ideas and recipes for it. Then, the next dash to put a meal on your table will be finished at record speed.

Acorn or Butternut Squash:
Mash and use in place of refried beans in tostados (see *Lifestyle for Health* cookbook, Mexican Squash Tostadas recipe).

Use in place of mashed potatoes as a side dish.

Add to muffins in place of applesauce.

Use in place of pumpkin in cakes or pies.

Use in soups (see *Lifestyle for Health* cookbook, Autumn Bisque recipe).

Cooked, mashed squash does freeze well. Freeze in 1/2 or 1 cup quantities. Extra can also be frozen in ice cube trays and then placed into plastic bags for storage.

Apples:
Cooked apples can be added to muffins and cakes (see *Lifestyle for Health* cookbook, Apple Cake). Add to pancakes (see LFH cookbook, Baked Apple Pancake recipe).

Cooked apples will freeze, but not raw apples. Apple pie can be frozen baked or unbaked (see this book, Apple Pie recipe, page 122).

Baked Potatoes:
While hot, mash into mashed potatoes (see *Lifestyle for Health* cookbook, Mashed Potato recipe). Grate and make into hash browns.

Mash and use as a crust for a veggie pie.

Layer them in a baked veggie casserole (see *Lifestyle for Health* cookbook, Veggie Casserole recipe).

Add to soups, i.e., vegetable soup.

Use in cream of potato soup or a chowder (see this cookbook, Broccoli Potato Soup recipe, page 43).

Mash filling and refill shells for twice baked potatoes (see this book, Twice Baked Potato recipe, page 159).

Raw potatoes do not freeze well. Twice baked potatoes do freeze well, as do most soups with potatoes.

Beans (i.e., legumes):
Mash and make refried beans and make tacos or burritos (see *Lifestyle for Health* cookbook, Refried Beans recipe).

Add to soups to thicken or as a soup (see this book, Black Bean recipe, page 36).

Use cooked pinto or mixed beans in baked beans (see *Lifestyle for Health* cookbook, Baked Bean recipe).

Toss into any green salad.

Add cooked, mashed beans to cakes or cookies (see *Lifestyle for Health* cookbook, Vonnie's Spice Cake recipe).

Cooked beans freeze well. Place in freezer bags and flatten contents. The thinner the bag, the faster the contents will thaw.

Biscuits or Muffins:
Crumble, toast and use as croutons or bread crumbs.

Extra muffins or biscuits freeze well. Cool and place in freezer bags. Take out as needed.

Broccoli:
Add to a shepherd or peasant pie (see this book, Leftover Vegetable Pie recipe, page 56, or *Lifestyle for Health* cookbook, Vegetable Deep–Dish Pie recipe).

Add to vegetable soup.

Use in cream of broccoli soup (see this book, Broccoli Potato Soup recipe, page 43).

Add to salads.

Add to pasta salads.

Raw broccoli does not freeze well. However, if it has been steamed or blanched, it will freeze. It will be somewhat limp, so it should be used in soups or casseroles.

Brown Rice:
Cool and use in fried rice (see this book, Fried Rice recipe, page 48).

Use in a rice salad (see this book, Rice Salad recipe, page 85).

Cool and use in Chili Rellenos (see this book, Chili Rellenos recipe, page 52).

Add to soups.

Mix with cooked beans to make a vegetarian patty.

Mix with tuna for tuna sandwiches. This extends the tuna; however, it is not the best food combining.

Use in rice pudding (see *Lifestyle for Health* cookbook, Rice Pudding recipe).

Use in casseroles (see *Lifestyle for Health* cookbook, Moussaka recipe).

Use in croquettes (see *Lifestyle for Health* cookbook, Tofu and Rice Croquettes).

Cooked rice does freeze, but it may be somewhat watery. It is fine for soup, pudding or casserole dishes.

Chicken:
Add to soups (see *Lifestyle for Health* cookbook, Cream of Chicken Soup recipe).

Use in salads (see *Lifestyle for Health* cookbook, Exotic Chicken Salad recipe).

Mix with veggies for chicken egg rolls (see *Lifestyle for Health* cookbook, Vietnamese Egg Roll recipe).

Make a chicken sandwich filling.

Add to a stir fry (see *Lifestyle for Health* cookbook, Chicken and Peanut Stir Fry recipe).

Use in a casserole (see *Lifestyle for Health* cookbook, Elaine's Chicken Jerusalem recipe).

Cooked chicken does freeze well.

Fruit:
Add to Fruit Smoothies.

Blend and use as a base for a dressing for a fruit salad.

Freeze grapes for 'mini' popsicles.

Freeze over–ripe bananas for Fruit Smoothies and baked goods. Freeze right in the skin and then run hot water over the frozen banana to loosen skin when ready to use. Frozen bananas will keep for several months.

Grains (whole grains, cooked):
Add to muffins, breads or cookies.

Add to soups.

Mix with veggies and add to soups.

Use to make croquettes.

Mix with mixed vegetables for a casserole.

Cooked grains do freeze well. They might become a little watery, so add them to soups, casseroles or other cooked dishes.

Gravy/Sauce:
Add to a vegetable pie (see *Lifestyle for Health* cookbook, Vegetable Deep–Dish Pie recipe).

Add to soups.

Lifestyle for Health cookbook and *Meals in 30 Minutes* recipes for Eggplant Pasta Sauce, Enchilada Sauce, Homemade Tomato Sauce, Mushroom Gravy, and the Cheese Sauce in Yellow Enchiladas freeze well. Place cooled sauce in zip–lock bags. Freeze flat. This container will thaw quickly.

Pasta:
Make a pasta salad by adding veggies, dressing and serve over lettuce.

Add to soups (see *Lifestyle for Health* cookbook, Escolata Soup recipe).

Soups:
Blend and use as an enhancement to most sauces.

Most soups freeze well. Freeze in small quantities for easy thawing and variety.

Use the Freezer and Multiply

A freezer is one of the easiest ways to have food ready in an instant. This chapter will help you purchase the right freezer for you, know what to do during and after power failure, know what foods freeze well and how long foods should be frozen before used. At the end of the chapter, you will find a few helpful hints on the use of a dehydrator, another method of food preservation.

Freezer Tips

The freezing compartment of a refrigerator is the least expensive freezer to buy. However, it is the most expensive to operate, provides the least cubic feet of freezing space and is not recommended for long–term storage since 0° is not too well maintained. (*Freeze With Ease* by Marion Fox Burros and Lois LeVine. Collier Book, NY, NY London page 3.)

Free–standing freezers come in two styles: chest or upright. The chest is least expensive to purchase and operate. The upright is more expensive, but more convenient and requires less floor space.

Take the time to purchase the right freezer for your needs. The right freezer can save you hours of time and provide great satisfaction when you pull a tasty, home–prepared meal from it's interior.

Power Failure

When you see a puddle of water around your freezer, it may be from some type of power failure. Before you panic, check out the following:

Was the door tightly shut? A door left ajar can cause a freezer to begin defrosting and food to thaw.

Has the freezer come unplugged? If so, plug it in.

Did a fuse blow? Reset the fuse.

If all of the above are OK, it is time to bring in a handyman or repairman.

At this point, keep the door tightly shut. Each "peek" causes precious cold air to escape. A fully stocked freezer will keep its contents frozen for at least two days (with the door tightly shut). A half–full freezer will last approximately one day.

If thawing does take place, there are also options. All uncooked foods may be cooked and refrozen. Baked goods may be refrozen, but they may be slightly drier when used.

According to the Department of Agriculture (House and Garden Bulletin #69), "If foods have thawed only partially and there are still ice crystals in the package, they may be safely refrozen." This will effect quality and texture.

The following tables gives you the suggested amount of time to store various foods in the freezer for maximum freshness.

FOOD	MAXIMUM MONTHS
Fruits and Vegetables:	
citrus fruits and juices	4 to 6
other fruits	8 to 12
vegetables	10
Baked Goods:	
bread, rolls, cakes	12
cookies	6 to 12
pies	6 to 12
pie shells	3
waffles and pancakes	6
Unbaked Goods:	
cake batter	1/2
cookie dough	3
Other:	
soups	4
nuts	12
combination dishes with meat	4 to 6
vegetarian combination dishes	6

Thawing

Thawing foods in their original wrapping in the refrigerator provides the best results, but it takes two to three times longer than thawing at room temperature. As a general rule, it takes six hours (in the fridge) per pound of food being defrosted. At room temperature, it requires approximately three hours.

Vegetables are best cooked while frozen. To grill frozen vegetables, let the veggies stand at room temperature for approximately three hours. Place the vegetables on a 12"

Creative Cooking: Use the Freezer and Multiply

square of heavy duty aluminum foil (I prefer to use parchment paper to avoid the alum in aluminum foil). Sprinkle with your favorite herbs. Cover with a second sheet of foil (or parchment paper) and seal the edges tightly. Cook 2 1/2" from heat for 30 to 35 minutes (turn halfway through).

Freezing No–No's
There are some foods that do not freeze well. Raw veggies (except for green peppers, cabbage and celery) should be blanched before freezing. Other foods that do not freeze well include:

hard–cooked eggs
boiled white potatoes
sour cream
melons
mayonnaise
stuffed poultry
jelly

Freezer Tips
Thaw, heat and serve frozen food in quick succession to prevent food spoilage.

Freeze food in moisture–proof, vapor–proof containers that have airtight seals. Glass, metal, rigid plastic, bags or freezer wrapping paper work well. Plain wax paper, commercial food containers (i.e. cottage cheese container), plastic product bags from the store and cellophane do not work as well.

Have store–bought pie crusts available in freezer for quick access (frozen whole wheat crusts are available in health food stores).

Packaging and Labeling

One of the most important steps to having quality frozen food is the packaging and labeling. Correct packaging can prevent discoloration, freezer burn, dehydration and poor thawed quality. When sealing, remove as much air as possible from the container to avoid freezer burn.

Be sure to label each freezer–bound package. Include contents, date and cooking directions, as well as number of servings. This will make using the contents much easier and faster at the time of use.

It is also helpful to freeze items based on a variety of quantities. For example, if you are a single person, freeze dishes in 1 to 2 serving sizes. If you are a family of four, freeze in 4 to 6 serving sizes. Freezing individual portions provides "instant" lunches for one or many. What a tasty, healthy treat, from your own freezer.

Dehydrators

Dehydrators remove the water from food, thereby making it lighter in weight, smaller in space and more concentrated. Drying makes use of food when it is abundant and less expensive. Dried food takes a fourth of the space of raw food. Fruit leathers are one of the most popular uses of dehydrators and very simple to make at home. (See the end of this chapter for recipes.)

If you do not have a dehydrator, an oven can be used for some items. Set the temperature at the lowest possible setting (or use just the lit pilot light). An oven will only allow for one or two shelves, whereas dehydrators can have four to twenty shelves.

Dehydrator Purchasing Tips

When purchasing a dehydrator, be sure to find a unit that has even heat distribution that will minimize or eliminate tray rotation. A temperature guide is necessary if you desire to make your own jerky or dried meats. Meats take a different temperature setting than fruits and vegetables.

The lower the temperature setting (i.e., about 98 degrees), the more nutrients will be saved in the food. Using a good dehydrator and good produce will eliminate the need for using any chemicals. I dry apples easily without any sulfur. Dried fruit in commercial stores are usually dried with sulfates to retain color.

Tips for Drying

Most vegetables, fruit, cooked meats and cottage cheese can be dried with excellent results. Most dehydrators will come with an instruction book giving details for their unit. Select ripe, cleaned produce. Slice produce into 1/8 to 1/4 inch thick slices. Have slices even for even drying.

Check produce as it dries so that it does not become over–dry.

Store dried food in air tight bags. They can then be frozen for even longer storage. Air–tight vacuum systems create the best environment for long–term storage. If it is humid, check for any bacteria. Dried foods will draw moisture from the air, so keep tightly sealed in small containers.

Grapes can be dried into raisins, but they may take longer than most fruits. Cranberries and blackberries do not dry well. Apples, apricots, blueberries, cherries, figs, huckleberries, peaches, pears, plums and melons dry well.

Greens, broccoli and potatoes do not dry well. Beans, beets, celery (in small pieces for soup), corn, okra, onions, carrots, parsnips, turnips, rutabagas, peppers, pumpkins, squash, sweet potatoes and herbs do dry well.

Vegetables that are lightly steamed keep better. They will also have a better appearance when dried.

Dark, cool places are best for dried foods.

Many dried foods are good eaten just as they are ... dry. However, to reconstitute, simply place dried vegetables in water and let soak 20 minutes to 2 hours, if possible. Then, cook until done. Soaking should occur in a refrigerator if soaked for longer than 2 hours to prevent spoilage. Dried fruits require one to eight hours to reconstitute when using cold water (less with hot water).

One cup of dried vegetables will reconstitute into about two cups, cooked. One cup of dried fruit will reconstitute into about 1 1/2 cups.

Dried vegetables can be ground in a good blender to make powders. A bushel of tomatoes, dried and ground can be stored in a one quart jar.

Homemade granola can be dried in a dehydrator or an oven (see *Lifestyle for Health* cookbook, Crunchy Granola recipe).

Freezer Recipes:
Twice Baked Potatoes
Bake large potatoes at 425 degrees until done when pierced with a fork.

Slice top off of each potato. Scoop out insides, leaving 1/4" sides (be sure not to cut all the way through).

Mash insides with milk (soy, rice or 2%), salt and butter (or canola oil or omit). Refill shell with mashed potato mixture. Freeze. Bake (frozen potato) at 350 degrees for 20 to 30 minutes or until done. (Can be topped with grated cheese or chives.)

Rice Pilaf
Follow recipe for Baked Rice Pilaf in *Lifestyle for Health* cookbook. (Add more liquid if rice becomes dry). Freeze. To serve, defrost and bake at 350 degrees for about 30 minutes.

Enchiladas
Freeze tortillas, filling and sauce separately (see *Kid's Favorites* cookbook, Yellow Enchiladas recipe). Defrost, assemble and bake.

Bierocks
An old German favorite. This is a great sandwich to pull out of the freezer, heat and eat.

> 1 pound whole grain bread dough
> 4–6 cups chopped cabbage
> 1 cup chopped onions
> 1 carrot, grated
> 1/2 tsp. sea salt or tamari, to taste
> 1/4 lb. ground meat or TVP
> 1/2 cup grated soy cheddar, optional

Sauté onion and cabbage in small amount of oil (garlic may also be added). Add meat or TVP, carrot and salt. Cook until veggies are tender. Cool and drain. (Mixture must be cool before placing on bread dough.) 1/2 cup soy cheddar can be added at this point.

Roll dough about 1/4 inch thick and cut into 4" squares. Place 1 heaping spoonful of filling on each square, pinch together tightly and place on greased pan with pinched sides down. Cover and let rise until double in size. Bake at 350 degrees for about 20 minutes or until done. These freeze well. To serve, place frozen bierock in preheated oven. Bake at 350 degrees for about 15 to 20 minutes or until heated through. Yields approximately 20 bierocks.

Dehydrator Recipes:
Dried Vegetable Soup

> 6 cups water
> 1/2 cup dried onions
> 1/4 cup dried peas
> 2 tbsp. dried parsley
> 1/2 cup grain*
> 1/2 cup dried carrots
> 1/2 cup dried celery
> 1 cup dried tomatoes
> 1/4 tsp. sage
> sea salt to taste, or tamari

Place vegetables in pot and cover with cold water. Bring to a boil, lower heat and simmer 4 to 6 hours until vegetables are tender. Adjust seasoning to taste.
> (* i.e., barley, brown rice or quinoa)

Salad Sprinkles
Dry diced onions, tomatoes, carrots and green pepper. Use the following amounts:

> 1/4 cup onion
> 1/4 cup tomatoes
> 1/4 cup carrots
> 1/4 cup green pepper

Creative Cooking: Use the Freezer and Multiply

Add 1/4 cup sunflower seeds, 2 tbsp. sesame seeds.
Mix all ingredients and use 1 tsp. on salads. Store extra in
refrigerator to retain crispness.

Zucchini Chippers
Before drying, sprinkle zucchini slices with sesame seeds
and garlic salt. Dry. Use as chips.

Fruit Leather
Puree various fruits (i.e., peaches, strawberries, bananas,
apples, etc.) in a blender or food processor with a little
water or juice. You can add some natural sweetener, but
ripe fruit rarely needs any more sweetening. Pour liquid
onto a fruit leather tray or a plastic–lined tray (this prevents
dripping onto other trays). Dry, roll up and store (or eat!).

Share the Fun With Friends

Four hands can make quick work of any job. Having a friend help you on your "sprint" cooking days can save time, double the food prepared and be fun. Select the friends you most enjoy working with. You may choose to work together or take turns baby–sitting young children for each other.

Older children can be helpful, if they have been taught how to help. Our daughter (at the age of 9) is a great help cleaning produce, stemming strawberries, cooking tortillas, etc. That extra pair of hands can be helpful, while building strong family relationships.

Co–ops

Along with working with a friend during bulk cooking, consider doing your food buying in a co–op or food buying club. A co–op or food buying club gives the recipients wholesale prices: usually 30 to 40% less than retail. This can be significant savings during bulk cooking or for families.

In the *Food Smart!* appendix, you will find wholesalers, listed by state. You can contact the wholesaler(s) nearest you to determine if there is a co–op or food buying club in your area. If there is no club, and you want to start your own, I recommend that you contact another club for start–up information.

Meal Sharing

Another way to do creative cooking with friends is to swap meals. Consider having four families participate in this venture. Plan out the types of meals that you all enjoy. Set a day aside to swap meals. If, for example, you pick Friday, Person A makes 4 meals on the first Friday. He/she coordinates the delivery to the other 3 families for their Friday meal. The next three Fridays, his/her family has their meal delivered to them.

This approach can be fun, if you plan. Be sure to take into consideration the various family members' likes and dislikes, family budgets, family sizes, work schedules and delivery logistics.

You may want to deliver meals during the day and have them heated at the last minute to avoid rush hour traffic. Or you may want to work with neighbors and deliver at the last minute.

The other variation of this theme is to have 2 to 3 families trade meals, but served in the host's home. For example, Person A cooks and serves in his/her home. Next week Person B cooks and serves in his/her home. This is less expensive than dining out and can be much more relaxing and enjoyable.

Sharing meals, whether it is the food, the fellowship or both, can be a wonderful way to make meal time enjoyable. Today's culture emphasizes convenience to the point of forgetting nourishment. Having a wonderful meal with friends is nourishing to the soul as well as the body.

Meals as Gifts

One of my favorite gifts to give and to receive is a home–cooked meal. For the person who has everything, a home–cooked meal is especially wonderful. For the harried mother of toddlers, a home–cooked meal is a slice of heaven. A fragrant, tasty home–cooked meal represents time, love and nurturing.

You can begin your holiday gift giving months in advance by placing extra meals in the freezer. I have presented many ideas in our *Gift Baskets* booklet. This booklet gives you many examples and recipes that are designed for gift giving.

Pasta is a very simple gift. Make homemade pasta, and freeze in bundles that fit into holiday tins. Add a pasta sauce to the pasta, place in a basket and Voila! — a perfect, quick gift. Or, make pizza crusts in single serving sizes. Place enough crusts for a family, along with some grated cheese, sauce and veggie toppings and you have a meal and a great gift.

Food makes a perfect gift for anybody anytime. When it comes in the form of a meal, it becomes even more perfect. Expand your creative bulk cooking to include friends, holidays and gifts. Your expanding culinary skills will be much appreciated.

Friends, food and fun. What a fulfilling way to live!

Nurture "Heart"
Healthy Cooking Skills

Cooking for Nourishment

So often I hear, "I wish I could eat at your house!" Many times that desire is expressed because of the variety and taste of our food. Just as our children's creativity is oftentimes eliminated by learning to perfectly "color within the lines," so many people have their culinary creativity bound by strict adherence to recipes.

Brilliant chefs are noted for their ability to cook without recipes. They understand food relationships, because they understand food is a source of nourishment and a means of expression. What you serve, how you serve it and the environment surrounding the meal all leads to total nourishment.

To nourish means to provide the substances necessary for life and growth. Although I am not an out–on–the–limb, strange person, I do believe that food prepared with love is much more nourishing than food prepared by a stranger who hates their job.

I can remember returning to my parents' home after a week of travel and hotel food. A simple soup and homemade bread tasted like heaven to my malnourished body. Why was that meal different? I had certainly been served soup and bread during my travels. The home–cooked meal was simple food prepared by loving hands and served in an environment of love and acceptance. What a difference that love made.

I can't explain how that transfusion happens, but I know it works. When I am upset about cooking, I am frustrated and the meal is mediocre at best. But when I take a little time, anticipate the fellowship of my family and/or friends, somehow the most humble of foods are elevated to the status of a feast.

If your meals seem humdrum and unappreciated, maybe the missing ingredient is love and generosity. Even the Proverbs expand on this truth (see Proverbs 23:6-8). God tells us that eating food from a person who is hard, grudging and envious will often make us vomit, or feel like it.

Take an inventory, private or public (as in asking your family). Do you cook solely because you have to? Sometimes, a meal seems only to be a necessity. However, how we prepare and serve the meal is a choice. I can choose to have a good attitude about serving my family or I can resent it. I can be frustrated that I am having guests or I can relish the opportunity to serve my friends.

Just as our faces often show our real emotions, so a meal shows our feeling about our family. I am not talking about the complexity or expense of a meal. I am talking about the heart–attitude of the person preparing the meal. Never underestimate how much you can nourish or malnourish by the attitude you entertain while preparing a meal. That particular pre–meal entertainment goes far into the actual meal.

How can you turn this attitude of "Oh, great! Another day, another meal!" around? I have found that as I give, so it is returned to me. When we generously give, we so generously reap many blessings. When I grudgingly give, I experience a grudging return. This law works without fail.

I have seen this happen over and over in my life. When I have the opportunity to prepare a meal, I always have a choice as to the attitude with which I prepare it. Does that mean I always do it right? No, but it does mean that when I have a lousy attitude, I'm not surprised when the meal is not the most enjoyable. On the other hand, when I take a few extra minutes, set the table extra nice or add some other considerate gesture, the meal goes so much more enjoyably.

True nourishment at a meal requires that you consider the heart. Not only should the meal be heart–healthy by avoiding the wrong foods, it must also be heart–healthy by avoiding the wrong attitudes.

Make a decision to learn how to begin to enjoy cooking. Take a class by someone who loves to cook. If you enjoy eating with friends, try a few potlucks and have everybody help out. If you are single, bored and lonely, try inviting a friend over for a simple bowl of soup.

Stepping outside of yourself and seeing the opportunity to give nourishment to others will reap a harvest of great nourishment in your body. Guaranteed! Plus, you will have so much more fun in the process than when you grudgingly threw a meal on the table. Try it and see for yourself.

Cooking as an Art
Many people look at cooking as a necessary evil based on stringent following of "the recipe." Recipes are only meant to be a starting point. I hardly ever follow any recipe, even

my own. I use a recipe as a starting place and then vary the ingredients based on what I have on hand.

For example, I may be in the mood for Italian and decide to use a package of polenta. I have extra chopped spinach, onion and mushrooms in the fridge. I have no recipe for all of these ingredients, so I start creating. I start by sautéing the onions and mushrooms. I broil several slices of polenta. I add the spinach to the mushrooms, with a little soy milk and parmesan cheese (soy or regular). Voila, I now top the polenta slices with my spinach mixture, sprinkle with a little mozzarella, broil until the cheese melts and I have a new Italian dish.

How did this dish happen? I used my experience (yes, that does take time and practice), along with the leftovers in my fridge to experiment. Does every dish turn out? No, but at this point they are usually at least edible. That skill comes from being willing to experiment and realize that some dishes will flop. That is how culinary creativity develops.

Learn to recognize the flavors that marry well (e.g., basil and tomato, poultry and sage, pumpkin and cinnamon, etc.). As you recognize this compatability and you have a few extra tomatoes, you automatically think of basil and Italian or salsa and Mexican.

As you become more experienced in compatible flavors, you will want to move out and try the exotic combinations. How about a stir fry with a curry seasoning? Maybe adding mashed beans to a cake batter will be interesting (see Vonnie's Spice Cake in the *Lifestyle for Health* cookbook). Now you are moving into the arena of a culinary chef. What fun cooking becomes as you allow your creativity to emerge and grow.

Variety is the Spice of Life

This book has presented techniques for bulk cooking, efficient use of a freezer and creative leftovers along with many recipes. This is comparable to a wardrobe of a variety of coordinating blouses, pants, skirts, dresses and jackets (or shirts, ties, pants and jackets). The well–dressed person knows how to mix and match to make that simple wardrobe *look* like a million dollars.

Likewise, the well–ordered chef (YOU) can learn how to mix and match the basics to make each meal *taste* like a million dollars. You won't want to bulk cook every recipe, or even cook once a month or week every time you cook. However, as you begin to intersperse these new techniques into your daily, weekly and monthly regime, you will begin to reduce the time in your kitchen. You will also begin to open many opportunities.... food to give to a new mother, extra food to share with best friends, a quick meal after an extra hard day at work or just your favorite foods only minutes away from the table ... all without a lot of fuss. This alone can help improve a person's attitude about cooking!

Begin by choosing just one of the techniques in this book. If you just read and think, "What a great idea," but never implement, that idea is a mere waste of ink and paper. If, instead, you begin to incorporate that great idea into your regular routine, the idea has formed a life of its own and will begin to bear fruit.

Start! Take a small step. Choose to learn to make cooking fun. Cook a few extra meals and share with friends. Camouflage those leftovers and surprise your family. You will be amazed at the difference such a plan can make in your life.

A heart of generosity kneaded with an ounce of opportunity and mixed with some yummy natural foods will produce a life that is fragrant, nourished and blessed. I do bless you with such a life.

PART III:

Resources

Supplementation

When my health collapsed (read *Food Smart!* for the whole story), we found two critical keys for the restoration of my health: cleansing and building. Cleansing is removing toxins (poisons) from the body. Building refers to strengthening the immune system and the overall defense systems in the body. A clean, strong body is healthy and resilient.

Both cleansing and building are often overlooked by people on the run. Fast, convenient foods are often full of chemicals and other toxin–producing elements while devoid of nutrition. If synthetic supplements are used, the problem may be simply multiplied. The body does not recognize foreign items, which most synthetic supplements are. The body recognizes food, preferably whole food, and supplements made from naturally derived food stuff.

The information contained in this section are a result of what has worked for our family and years of research. It is not intended to replace a health care provider or to be used as a prescription. Please consult your health care provider for any personal application.

Cleansing

Since *Food Smart!* addresses many specific cleanses in detail, we will not recover that information here. However, here are some basic cleanses that can be helpful as starting places. We use them on a regular basis.

Pure water, fruits and vegetables are components of a basic cleanse often referred to as a Daniel Fast. During periods of high stress, we often limit our food intake to these easily digested, energy–loaded foods. Be sure produce is organic or washed in a preparation that removes as many oil–based pesticides as possible (Shaklee Basic H is our preference).

Key times to consider cleansing include: during stress, after travel, in the spring or after periods of medication. Cleansing is similar to cleaning a physical house. Cleaning can be deep cleaning (usually only about once a year), weekly cleaning or a quick wipe here and there. Body cleansing can follow these same patterns. From a casual cleansing bath (see *Food Smart!)* to a spring detox, your health care provider can help you customize a cleansing program that will help you on an ongoing basis keep your body clean and healthy.

A couple of products that we have found helpful are produced by UltraBalance, Inc. called UltraClear™ and UltraClear Sustain™. These products are designed to be used in combination with a low–allergy or food–elimination and reintroduction diet. To provide protein of high biological value and low allergy potential, these UltraClear™ products contain a special amino acid–fortified rice–protein concentrate as their only protein source.

We have found that these products work well as an addition to our daily fruit smoothie drink. They add nutrition, energy and taste to our drink. They help provide nutrients to our gastrointestinal cells, thereby supporting the growth of desirable (or "friendly") bacteria.

UltraClear Sustain™ helps eliminate gastrointestinal parasites and/or other undesirable bacteria. It also helps replace digestive factors (e.g., enzymes) you may be lacking. UltraClear™ supports the body's natural detoxification processes. Detox occurs primarily in the liver and gastrointestinal cells, which UltraClear™ addresses. For further information on these excellent products, please call the Metagenics office at (303) 371–6848.

Lifestyle for Health has joined with a manufacturer to produce a cleanser called Accent Life (L´) 3–D Cleanser. This cleanser, in a base of aloe and cranberry juice, contains herbs, minerals and other nutrients. The added nutrients include:

Choline (helps assimilate fat and cholesterol, prevents fat accumulation in the liver, cleans kidneys),

Inositol (helps with fat metabolism, reduction of blood cholesterol, prevention of fatty hardening of arteries and improves brain cell nutrition),

Watermelon seeds (used to dissolve kidney stones) as well as many other nutrients.

The primary function of the 3–D Cleanser is to help pull cholesterol from the blood, remove fat from the liver, cleanse the kidneys and colon — basically, clean the body's plumbing system. Call the Lifestyle for Health office at (303) 771–9357 for order information on this cleanser.

Cleansing has been a key to my continually improving health. You may want to consider it as a basic foundation along with quality supplements and whole foods for ongoing good health.

Supplements
"Nutrition is the relationship of foods to the health of the human body. Proper nutrition means that all the essential

nutrients — that is carbohydrates, fats, protein, vitamins, minerals, and water — are supplied and utilized in adequate balance to maintain optimal health and well–being. Nutritional deficiencies result whenever inadequate amounts of essential nutrients are provided to tissues that must function normally over a long period of time. Good nutrition is essential for normal organ development and functioning, for normal reproduction, growth and maintenance, for optimum activity level and working efficiency; for resistance to infection and disease; and for the ability to repair bodily damage or injury.

"No single substance will maintain vibrant health. Although specific nutrients are known to be more important in the functions of certain parts of the body, even those nutrients are totally dependent upon the presence of other nutrients for their best effects. Every effort should therefore be made to attain and maintain an adequate, balanced daily intake of all the necessary nutrients throughout life." [1] *Nutrition Almanac* Third Edition, by Lavon J. Dunne, McGraw Hill, Publishing Company, NY, NY, 1990.

The *Nutrition Almanac* is an excellent resource for various nutrients and the deficiencies associated with many ailments. It can become a handy reference guide for addressing many nutritional questions.

Since overall health is dependent upon a well–balanced diet, it is imperative to eat a variety of fresh fruits, vegetables, whole grains, legumes and seeds. When under extra stress (which quickly depletes nutrients), traveling or other specific times, supplements may be needed to augment a natural diet. The following supplements are ones we have found helpful at different times.

Enzymes
We all know that we need five servings of fruit and
vegetables a day, but how many of us do it? And, of that
intake, most of it should be in a raw form to provide
enzymes. Enzymes are the active materials found in the
digestive system that allow nutrients to be absorbed and
assimilated. Enzymes are to the body as spark plugs are to a
car — they unlock energy and movement. It is not just the
food you eat, but what you assimilate and absorb in that
food that produces health.

The high intake of refined food, lacking in enzymes,
I believe to be one of the leading causes of malnutrition in
America. This malnutrition leads to a broken immune
system and the resulting list of immune deficient diseases
that face our society.

A regular intake of enzymes has been a regular part
of our supplementation (including our daughter). We have
found two enzyme products on the market that are helpful
in ensuring your daily intake. Either product helps ensure
that you are getting your daily five servings of fruits and
vegetables with live, not dead, enzymes. Juice Plus is a
product that has been around for several years and is
distributed through NSA.

Lifestyle for Health has developed an enzyme
product through Accent Life (L´) called Vegetable and Fruit
Concentrate. The special flash drying process used
eliminates the water, leaving a powerful enzyme and fiber
concentrate from fruit and vegetable juices.

Multi Vitamins
We have found a multi vitamin to be a good foundation for
us. It is key that the vitamins be joined with minerals for

optimum absorption. It is also critical that the vitamins and minerals not be synthetic (foreign to the body). Check the label to ensure that the product is made without added sugar, starch, artificial colors or flavors.

We have found the following brands produce quality, natural supplements: NeoLife, Shaklee, Amway, Nature's Way and Maleleuca. Lifestyle for Health has a MultiVitamin and Mineral through our supplement line, Accent Life (L'). Call our office at (303) 771–9357 for order information.

Some of the specific vitamins and minerals may be needed in higher doses for specific reasons. Some of those vitamins and minerals are listed below.

Vitamin A
Vitamin A, a fat–soluble nutrient (fat–soluble requires presence of bile salts and fat for absorption), is converted from carotene (rich in carrots and leafy green vegetables). Vitamin A aids in the growth and repair of body tissues and maintenance of disease–free skin. It also helps reduce sensitivity to infections, aids in the digestion of protein and helps build strong teeth and bones. The RDA (recommended daily allowance) for Vitamin A is 1500–4000 IU's for children and 4000–5000 IU's for adults (more during disease, trauma, pregnancy and lactation.

Vitamin B
Vitamin B has long been called the stress vitamin. Vitamin B is actually a complex of many water soluble nutrients that can be cultivated from bacteria, yeasts, fungi or molds. This complex helps provide the body with energy, fat metabolism, a healthy nervous system and healthy skin,

hair, eyes, mouth and liver. All of the B vitamins can be found in Brewer's yeast, liver and whole–grain products.

Being a water soluable nutrient, it is not stored and must be replenished regularly. High alcohol and sugar intake often produces a Vitamin B deficiency. The RDA varies for each of the 13 or more B–complex vitamins.

Vitamin C

Vitamin C, a water–soluble vitamin, is linked to maintaining collagen (formation of smooth skin and strong ligaments and bones). It also plays a role in the healing of wounds, burns and scars. Vitamin C helps prevent hemorrhaging, fights bacterial infections and reduces the effects of allergy–producing substances. It is the common fighter of the common cold.

During high periods of stress, the adrenal glands rapidly use up adrenal ascorbic acid. Iron absorption is also increased with adequate Vitamin C. The RDA for Vitamin C is 60 mg. for adults. A timed–release remedy with bioflavonoids is considered to be more helpful.

Vitamin E

Vitamin E is a fat–soluble vitamin (fat–soluble requires presence of bile salts and fat for absorption) and an antioxidant (fights free radicals, a precursor of cancer). As both a supplement or ointment, it helps prevent scar formation. As a diuretic, it helps lower elevated blood pressure and protects against environmental toxins. Research appears to link Vitamin E with calcium metabolism, correcting too high or low deposits.

It is usually advised that iron and Vitamin E be taken separately for maximum absorption. Chlorinated drinking water, rancid oils, mineral oil and added estrogen all increase the depletion of Vitamin E. Vitamin E is primarily found in grains, oils and nuts; however, the amounts are small. An added Vitamin E supplement is often advised.

Calcium
Soft drinks leach calcium from the body. If you are drinking them, add calcium in the form of supplementation.

Chromium
Chromium is an essential mineral that is an active ingredient in a substance called GTF (Glucose Tolerance Factor). Chromium aids in the metabolism of glucose for energy and the assimilation of fatty acids and cholesterol. It appears to increase the effectiveness of insulin and, as such, can be helpful to diabetics.

The foods that contain chromium (in a form that can be assimilated) include Brewer's yeast, liver, beef, whole–wheat bread, beets, molasses and mushrooms. Increased chromium has also been linked to weight loss due to better metabolism of sugar. Accent Life (L′) has a chromium supplement. Call the Lifestyle for Health office at (303) 771–9357.

Zinc
Zinc is one of the largest occurring trace minerals found in the body. It aids in the absorption of vitamins (especially B, therefore it has a link to stress), breakdown of alcohol and digestion of carbohydrates. Zinc is critical for normal functioning of the prostate gland and is often take in additional amounts by men with a tendency toward prostate cancer.

The RDA for zinc is 15 mg. for adults (extra during pregnancy and lactation). Additional A is recommended when taking extra zinc. High levels of alcohol, stress and fatigue can lead to zinc deficiency. A lack of zinc is also associated with white spots on fingernails, brittle nails and hair, irregular menstrual cycles and sterility. Zinc can be found in whole–grain products, Brewer's yeast, wheat bran, wheat germ and pumpkin seeds or as a supplement.

Flaxseed oil

Flaxseed oil is rich in Essential Fatty Acids. EFA's cannot be manufactured by the body, so they must come from diet or supplementation. They are important for oxygen transportation, cell lubrication and solidarity, blood coagulation rates, cholesterol breakdown and normal thyroid and adrenal gland activity.

Flaxseed oil is an excellent source of EFA's and the omega–3 oils. It is a vegetarian option to fish oils. I highly recommend the Spectrum or Rohé brands of flaxseed oil. Flax oil is highly sensitive to light and heat, so be sure to check pressing dates (seek current dates) and store in the refrigerator. Additional Vitamin E is recommended when taking flaxseed oil.

Garlic

Garlic has been used to treat disease for many years. It is a strong antiviral, antibacterial and antifungal herb. We have found that, when taken regularly, garlic helps prevent colds and other viral illnesses. Garlic also helps build a strong immune system, which can aid in preventing immune system disorders, such as cancer.

I highly recommend Kyolic for garlic products. Their aged garlic extract is an excellent product that we add daily to our fruit smoothie drink. Kyolic is available in most health food stores throughout the country.

Milk Thistle

Milk thistle is an herb that is noted for building a strong, clean liver. It can block the damage and regenerate the liver cells. It is also an antioxidant and protects against free radicals and thereby helps strengthen the immune system.

Milk thistle can be found in either a tincture (liquid) or dry form. I add several drops to my morning fruit smoothie to help with liver building. A tea can also be made from the dry leaf.

Arnica

Arnica is a homeopathic alternative to aspirin. We have found it helpful for pain and muscle tenderness. Several excellent homeopathic brands exist. Follow the manufacturer directions for dosage.

Echinacea

Echinacea is an herb that stimulates the immune response, thereby increasing the body's ability to resist infections. It is considered one of the best blood purifiers and helpful for enlarged or weakened prostate glands. We combine echinacea with goldenseal (we have found we prefer it in a tincture form) to fight any cold or flu symptoms. Follow the manufacturer directions for dosage.

Lecithin

Lecithin is a natural component of every human cell and helps to emulsify cholesterol. It works with iron, iodine and calcium to invigorate the brain and help digest and absorb fats. It has also been linked to the prevention of atherosclerosis, prevention of the formation of gallstones and even weight distribution. Lecithin also helps cleanse the liver and purify the kidneys.

Two tablespoons a day are recommended. It comes in both a powdered and a liquid form. Lecithin is found naturally in egg yolks, liver, nuts, soybeans, whole wheat and corn.

Evening of Primrose Oil
EPO is another essential fatty acid that is linked to helping with many female problems.

It has been found to help in the regulating of menstrual cycles. It is high in the omega–6 oils (GLA or gamma–linolenic acid). Additional Vitamin E is recommended when taking primrose oil.

KyoGreen
KyoGreen is a green powder, rich in minerals, manufactured by Kyolic. It contains chlorophyll–rich nutrients from land and sea vegetables. Chlorophyll is an excellent blood and colon cleaner. It is also good for children and nursing mothers. We add a teaspoon per person to our morning fruit smoothie drink.

Acidophilus
Acidophilus is important to take after the use of antibiotics, which destroy healthy bacteria in the intestine. Kyolic makes an excellent acidophilus, which is heat stabilized, thereby not needing to be refrigerated.

Summary
This is in no way meant to be an exhaustive list of supplements. However, it is a list of basics that many people have found to be helpful. As you work with a health care practitioner, educate yourself and learn how your body responds, you will be able to develop a regular regime that works for you.

We have found that our regime varies from season to season, from year to year and with special needs. Your body changes constantly, so be prepared to vary your supplements as needed.

If you are under stress, eating on the run or eating a highly refined diet, you are in a critical health crunch. Learning how to improve your food intake and using the appropriate supplements may save your life.

Substitutions and Equivalents

Fruit Equivalents:
Apples: 3 medium = 1 lb. = 3 c. sliced

Bananas: 3 medium = 1 lb. = 2 c. sliced = 1 c. mashed

Dates: 1 lb. = 3 c. chopped

Lemon: 1 medium = 2 to 3 tbsp. juice, 2 tsp. lemon zest

Lime: 1 medium = 1 1/2 to 2 tbsp. juice, 1 tsp. lime zest

Orange: 1 medium = 1 1/2 c. juice, 2 tsp. orange zest

Peach: 1 medium = 1 1/2 c. sliced

Pear: 1 medium = 1 1/2 c. sliced

Raisins: 1 lb. = 3 c.

Strawberries: 1 qt. = 4 c. sliced

Grain Equivalents:
Cornmeal: 1 lb. = 3 c.

Flaked cereal: 3 c. dry = 1 c. crushed

Oats: 1 c. = 1 3/4 c. cooked

Rice: 1 c. = 3 to 4 c. cooked

Nut Equivalents:
Almonds: 1 lb. unshelled = 1 3/4 c. nutmeat
           1 lb. shelled = 3 1/2 c. nutmeat

Peanuts: 1 lb. unshelled = 1 3/4 c. nutmeat
           1 lb. shelled = 3 1/2 c. nutmeat

Pecans: 1 lb. unshelled = 1 3/4 c. nutmeat
           1 lb. shelled = 3 1/2 c. nutmeat

Walnuts: 1 lb. unshelled = 1 3/4 c. nutmeat
           1 lb. shelled = 3 1/2 c. nutmeat

Vegetable Equivalents:
Cabbage: 1 lb. = 3 c. shredded

Corn: 2 medium ears = 1 c. kernels

Mushrooms: 8 oz. = 3 c. raw = 1 c. sliced, cooked

Onion: 1 medium = 1/2 c. chopped

Pepper, green: 1 large = 1 c. diced

Potato (sweet): 3 medium = 3 c. sliced

Potato (white): 3 medium = 2 c. cubed, cooked = 1 3/4 c. mashed

Other Equivalents:
Carob chips: 12 oz. = 2 c.

Carob powder: 1 lb. = 4 c.

Coconut: 1 lb. = 5 c. flaked or shredded

Milk cheese, raw: 1 lb. = 4 c. shredded

Pasta: 4 oz. = 1 c. = 2 1/4 c. cooked

General Equivalents:

3 tsp. = 1 tbsp.

16 fluid oz. = 2 c. = 1 pt.

2 tbsp. (liquid) = 1 oz.

1/8 c. = 2 tbsp.

4 tbsp. = 1/4 c.

5 1/3 tbsp. = 1/3 c.

8 tbsp. = 1/2 c.

16 tbsp. = 1 c.

8 fluid oz. = 1 c.

1/3 c. = 5 tbsp. + 1 tsp.

2/3 c. = 10 tbsp. + 2 tsp.

4 c. = 1 qt.

4 qts. = 1 gal.

Substitutes:

Baking powder: two parts cream of tartar, one part baking soda and two parts arrowroot

Bread crumbs: toasted oats, sesame seeds, cooked brown rice or other cracked grains

Butter: in baking, canola oil, safflower oil, sunflower oil or applesauce (up to 1/2 c. per recipe)

> 1 tbsp. = 1 tsp. light miso plus 2 tsp. olive oil for mashed potatoes

Buttermilk: 1 c. = 1 c. minus 1 tbsp. of soy milk, rice milk or almond milk, plus 1 tbsp. lemon juice

Cheese: equal amounts of soy or almond cheeses.

Cheese, cottage cheese:

> 1 lb. firm tofu, mashed
> 1 tbsp. olive oil
> 1 tbsp. rice or apple-cider vinegar
> 2 tbsp. lemon juice
> 1/4 to 1/2 tsp. onion powder, to taste
> 1/4 to 1/2 tsp. salt or tamari, to taste
>
> Mix half of tofu and remaining ingredients in blender. Mix in remaining mashed tofu.

Cheese, cream cheese = "yo" cheese: Strain yogurt in yogurt strainer, or coffee filter placed in strainer, for 24 hours (set in refrigerator while draining).

Cheese, ricotta:

> 1 lb. firm tofu, mashed
> 1/4 c. olive oil
> 1/2 tsp. nutmeg
> 1/2 tsp. salt or tamari
>
> Mix half of tofu and remaining ingredients in blender. Mix in remaining tofu.

Chicken: (This tip was provided us by Morinaga, manufacturers of Mori Nu Tofu.) Slice one package of Mori Nu Extra Firm Tofu, "lite" into four horizontal slices. Freeze in a single layer. Thaw and squeeze out excess liquid. Marinate in a sauce for 30 minutes or more. Cook according to the individual recipe's directions.

Chocolate: 1 square or 1 oz. = 3 tbsp. carob plus 1 tbsp. oil and 1 tbsp. water

Cocoa: 1 c. = 1 c. carob powder

Cornstarch: 1 tbsp. = 1 tbsp. arrowroot powder

Cream, heavy: 1 tbsp. tahini dissolved in 1/4 c. water (this will not whip)

Cream, sour: "yo" cheese or equal amount of soft tofu

Currants: raisins

Eggs: one egg =

> 1 tbsp. soy flour
> 1 tbsp. water plus 1 tbsp. powdered soy lecithin
> commercial egg replacer
> half of a ripe banana
> 4 oz. firm tofu
> 1/4 c. applesauce
> 1/4 c. "yo" cheese

Flour, white (as sauce thickener): 1 tbsp. = 1/2 tbsp. arrowroot

Flour, white (in baking):

> 1 c. = 1 c. corn flour
> 1 c. = 3/4 c. coarse cornmeal
> 1 c. = 7/8 c. rice flour
> 1 c. = 1 c. spelt flour
> 1 c. = 1 c. kamut flour
> 1 c. = 1/2 c. barley flour + 1/4 c. rice flour + 1/2
> tbsp. arrowroot powder

Garlic: 1 clove =

> 1 tsp. minced garlic
> 1/2 tsp. garlic powder

Milk: 1 c. = 1 c. almond milk, soy milk, rice milk or 1 c. water plus 1 tbsp. tahini, mixed

Milk, sour: 1 c. = 1 tbsp. lemon juice or vinegar plus 1 c. less 1 tbsp. milk. Let set 5 minutes.

Pan preparation: lightly oil or brush with lecithin mixture (6 tbsp. canola, 2 tbsp liquid lecithin — mix well).

Pepper: 1 tsp. black pepper = 1/4 tsp. cayenne

Sugar, brown:

> 1 c. = 1/2 c. date sugar and 1/2 c. honey
> 1 c. = 1/2 to 3/4 c. honey
> 1 c. = 3/4 c. maple syrup
>
> (use 1/2 c. less liquid per cup sweetener and reduce oven temperature by 25 degrees)

Sugar, white:

> 1 c. = 1 c. FruitSource
> 1 c. = 3/4 c. to 1 c. Sucanat
> 1 c. = 3/4 c. maple syrup (use 2 tbsp. less liquid in recipe)
> 1 c. = 3/4 c. honey (use 2 tbsp. less liquid per cup of honey used and lower oven temperature by 25 degrees)
> 1 c. = 1 c. rice syrup
> 1 c. = 1 c. molasses plus 1/2 tsp. baking soda (use 1/4 c. less recipe liquid per 1 c. of molasses)

Worcestershire sauce: 3 tbsp. = 1/4 c. tamari

Yogurt: equal amount of tofu

Preferred Brands

When a person begins to change what he or she eats, one of the most overwhelming jobs is grocery shopping. The familiar brands go by the wayside. But how does one begin to shop for new brands? Our family has found the following brands taste good, are reasonably priced and contain quality ingredients. It is important to support companies that are committed to quality products — to do our part.

This list is not all–inclusive, but it does contain the brands we use on a regular basis. I am sure you will find these brands to be a good starting place. No company has paid for these recommendations. I am simply passing on our preferences after years of experimentation.

If you are unable to find these products in your store, you may want to ask that they carry them. Some companies allow you to order directly. Many have free recipe booklets and product brochures.

Alta Dena has a great line of quality dairy products, from fresh milk to kefir, yogurt, ice cream and others. They are committed to producing milk products without bovine growth hormones. Dairy products without this hormone are much safer for you and your family. Alta Dena's quality and integrity are excellent.

> Alta Dena Certified Dairy
> P.O. Box 388
> City–Industry, CA 91747–0388

(818)964–6401
(800)535–1369

Annie's produces excellent dressings and barbecue sauces. Their dressings and sauces are just like homemade — fresh and tasty. Try their barbecue sauce on oven–fried potatoes. The raspberry dressing is one of our family's favorites.

Annie's
Foster Hill Road
North Calais, VT 05650
(802)456–8866

Arrowhead Mills is a wonderful manufacturer that will easily replace many all–purpose brands that you currently purchase. Virtually all their products are organic with great taste and include whole grains, flours, mixes, beans, seeds, nut and seed butters (they have excellent tahini), oils, flakes and soup mixes.

Arrowhead Mills, Inc.
110 South Lawton
Box 2059
Hereford, TX 79045
(806)364–0730

Barbara's Bakery provides quality, nutritious foods, from chips, pretzels and cookies to cereals, granola bars, bread sticks and crackers. Their food is tasty and very reasonably priced. Many low–fat and no–fat foods are available.

Barbara's Bakery, Inc.
3900 Cypress Drive
Petaluma, CA 94954
(707)765–2273

Cascadian Farms provides a wealth of excellent products. Many of their products are organic, from their frozen fruits and vegetables to their jams, jellies, preserves, sorbets, pickles and relishes. They have great "popsicles" made with organic milk and unrefined sugar. Kosher foods are also available.

> Cascadian Farms
> P.O. Box 568
> Concrete, WA 98237
> phone: (206)855–0100
> fax: (206)855–0444

Celestial Seasonings produces the finest line of herbal teas. They now have a line of black teas and gourmet after–dinner teas. Any of their teas mix well with fresh fruit juices for a delightful option.

> Celestial Seasonings
> 4600 Sleepytime Drive
> Boulder, CO 80020
> (303)530–5300

Cold Mountain Miso (white miso) can be found in the dairy sections of most health food stores. The lighter the color of the miso, the milder the flavor. Miso is a great replacement for traditional bouillon cubes.

> Cold Mountain Miso
> Miyako Oriental Foods Inc.
> 4287 Puente Avenue
> Baldwin Park, CA 91706
> phone: (818)962–9633
> fax: (818)814–4569

Coleman Natural Meats come from cattle that are totally natural and raised without hormones or steroids. The flavor is excellent, beyond comparison to other commercially available meats. They provide beef and some other meats.

> Coleman Natural Meats Inc.
> 5140 Race Court #4
> Denver, CO 80127
> phone: (303)297–9393
> fax: (303)297–0426

DeBoles Pasta is a good transition pasta for families just beginning to change their diet. These pastas are made with semolina and Jerusalem artichoke flour. They also provide some corn pasta and other bakery products. This pasta is much lighter than white flour pasta and comes in many varieties.

> DeBoles Nutritional Foods, Inc.
> 2120 Jericho Turnpike
> Garden City Park, NY 11040
> (516)742–1818

Devan Soy Farms, Inc. has an outstanding soy beverage product line. Their natural granular sweetener line, based on brown rice, is also first–rate.

> Devan Soy Farms, Inc.
> P.O. Box 885
> Carroll, IA 51401
> (800)747–8605

Eden produces excellent vinegars, along with many other Asian foods, tomato products, pastas, beans and soy milks. Many products are organic. Their brand names include Eden, Edensoy and Herbs Pasta.

Eden Foods, Inc.
701 Tecumseh
Clinton, MI 49236
(517)456–7424

Fantastic Foods has one of the best lines of packaged foods. They produce natural convenience food (dry mixes), grains, cereals and soups. They also have kosher foods. Their brand names include Fantastic Falafel, Nature's Burger (great vegetarian hamburger replacement), Quick Pilafs, Instant Refried Beans, Fantastic Noodles and Meals In A Cup.

Fantastic Foods
1250 North McDowell Boulevard
Petaluma, CA 94954
(707)778–7801

Frontier provides fresh herbs in bulk and packaged forms. They also produce organic coffees. This company is committed to quality and integrity.

Frontier Cooperatives Herbs
1 Frontier Road
P.O. Box 299
Norway, IA 52318
(800)669–3275

FruitSource is a balanced sweetener made from brown rice and grapes that some diabetics can use. It comes in both liquid and granular forms. It can be used one for one in sugar replacement. Due to its humectancy, fat in recipes using FruitSource should be reduced. Check the FruitSource label for guidelines.

FruitSource
1803 Mission Street, #404
Santa Cruz, CA 95060
(408)457–1136

Garden of Eatin' has a wide variety of chips. I have found
that many people do better with the blue or red corn chips
instead of the yellow. They also have excellent pita breads,
bagels, tortillas, chapatis and sprouted rolls. Certified
organic ingredients are included in most products.

Garden of Eatin'
5300 Santa Monica Boulevard
Los Angeles, CA 90029
(213)462–5406

Glenny's produces an alternative to candy with sugar. From
lollipops to snack bars, their products are a great alternative.
Brand names include Nookies, Noah 'N Friends Animal
Cookies and Glenny's.

Glenny's 100% Natural Snacks
999 Central Avenue
Woodmere, NY 11598
(no phone listed)

Grape Vine Trading Company has a full line of natural
dried foods, specializing in native California produce. Look
to them for variously flavored tapeande, sun–dried
tomatoes, wild mushrooms, spices and various California
products — rices, organic garlic and dried fruits and much
more. Write or call them for a free product brochure.

Grape Vine Trading Company
59 Maxwell Court
Santa Rosa, CA 95401
phone: (707)576–3950
fax: (707)576–3945

Guiltless Gourmet has excellent fat–free snacks including baked, no–oil chips. Their fat–free bean dips and salsas are excellent and some of our favorites.

Guiltless Gourmet
3709 Promontory Point Drive, Suite 131
Austin, TX 78744
(512)443–4373

Hatch provides great Mexican foods, from salsas to chilies, refried beans (both pinto and black bean), and taco shells. Their green chili enchilada sauce (vegetarian) is excellent.

Hatch Chili Company
P.O. Box 752
Deming, NM 88031
(505)546–4298

Imagine Foods makes three delicious brands, including Rice Dream, Ken & Robert's and Veggie Pockets. Rice Dream is a food product made from the starch portion of brown rice. It is a delicious milk that can be used for drinking, cooking and baking. It is also available in frozen "ice–cream" type products. Ken & Robert's is a brand of delicious frozen vegetarian entrees. Veggie Pockets are frozen vegetarian pocket sandwiches, individually frozen for quick meals.

Imagine Foods
350 Cambridge Avenue, #350
Palo Alto, CA 94306
phone: (415)327–1444
fax: (415)327–1459

Knudsen & Sons has great juices, carbonated beverages, syrups and spreads. Their products are an excellent replacement for sugar–sweetened colas and carbonated beverages.

Knudsen & Sons
P.O. Box 369
Chico, CA 95927
(916)891–1517

Kyolic products have become a daily staple in our home. From Kyolic (aged garlic) to KyoGreen, we use each product to build our immune system and help maintain overall strong body systems. KyoGreen is added to our fruit smoothies each morning. Kyolic garlic is a regular supplement throughout the year, especially during the fall and winter. KyoDophilus (acidophilus) is used to balance intestinal flora — especially important after using antibiotics or having colonics.

Wakunuaga of America Co., Ltd.
23501 Madero
Mission Viejo, CA 92691
(714)855–2776

Lundberg produces organic and premium brown–rice products. They also have rice blends, brown–rice cakes, flours, cereals and pilafs. Their brown–rice syrup is an excellent sugar replacement that many diabetics can use.

Their brown–rice pudding mixes are excellent, as are their one–step chili mixes.

Lundberg Family Farms
P.O. Box 369
Richvale, CA 95974
(916)882–4551

Maine Coast Sea Vegetables offers a full line of sea vegetables or seaweed. Adding that strip of kombu to your soups or beans aids in digestion and intake of minerals.

Maine Coast Sea Vegetables
Shore Road
Franklin, MA 04630
(207)565–2907

Mom's Spaghetti Sauce is one of our all–time favorite sauces on our homemade pasta. It has big chunks of fresh basil and whole cloves of garlic. A truly delicious sauce.

Mom's Spaghetti Sauce
Timpone's Fresh Foods Corp.
3211 Thornton B
Austin, TX 78704
(512)442–7772

Mori Nu has the best silken tofu (a smooth tofu with the texture of sour cream, without the cholesterol). It works the best with many of my recipes. It comes in aseptic packaging for longer shelf life. Their "lite" tofu has the least amount of fat of any tofu on the market.

Mori Nu
2050 West 190th, #110
Torrance, CA 90504

phone: (800)NOW TOFU
fax: (310)787–2727

Mountain Sun is committed to organic products. They provide great organic and natural food juices under the labels of Mountain Sun and Apple Hill. Their flavors and varieties are superb.

Mountain Sun
18390 Hwy. 145
Dolores, CO 81323
phone: (303)882–2283
fax: (303)882–2270

Muir Glen tomato products are by far my favorite. These organically grown tomato products are packaged in enamel lined cans, which produces a superior taste and product. Their products range from chunky sauces to paste to whole tomatoes. Throw away those tinny–tasting tomatoes and try Muir Glen.

Muir Glen
424 North 7th Street
Sacramento, CA 95814
phone: (800)832–6345
fax: (916)557–0903

Nayonaise produces a dairy–free mayo made from tofu. They also make tofu dressings, wonton skins, egg roll wrappers and tofu.

Nasoya Foods Inc.
23 Jytek Drive
Leominster, MA 01453
(508)537–0713

Nest Eggs provides eggs from uncaged hens that are fed a drug–free diet. Quality eggs are just as important as organic grains, produce and meats.

> Nest Eggs Inc.
> P.O. Box 14599
> Chicago, IL 60614
> (no phone listed)

Pamela's Products produces our favorite cookies. Many of their cookies are wheat–free (wheat is the most common American food allergy), sugar–free and some are dairy–free. A line of biscotti cookies has been added to the regular line.

> Pamela's Products
> 156 Utah Avenue
> South San Francisco, CA 94080
> (415)952–4546

Parsley Patch provides an excellent line of salt–free seasonings. Their Mexican Blend is a staple for my Mexican dishes.

> Parsley Patch
> McCormick & Co., Inc.
> Hunt Valley, MD 21031–1100
> (410)771–7301

Roaster Fresh makes excellent nut butters. They are produced by Kettel Foods, which also makes chips, popcorn and other nuts and seeds.

> Roaster Fresh/Kettle Foods
> P.O. Box 664
> Salem, OR 97308
> (503)364–0399

Rohé Natural Products includes a full line of minimally processed oils in quality containers.

> Rohé Natural Products
> 15810 Shawnee Circle
> Middletown, CA 95461
> (707)928–4098

San–J has great sauces for stir–fries and marinades. Their tamari has an excellent flavor and will quickly replace your sodium–laden soy sauces. Their Thai peanut sauce is great for stir–fries and in salads. Their miso soup (I prefer the mild) is a delicious cup–a–soup.

> San–J International, Inc.
> 2880 Sprouse Drive
> Richmond, VA 23231
> (804)226–8333

Sharon's Finest produces Rella, a line of soy cheeses for those with dairy sensitivities. All Rella cheeses work great as alternatives to dairy–based cheese. Rella melts well and has good flavor. They have many varieties in their line.

> Sharon's Finest
> P.O. Box 5020
> Santa Rosa, CA 95402
> (707)576–7050

Shelton products, poultry, are raised without antibiotics and are free–range grown. They are also raised without hormones, or growth stimulants, which are common in most other commercially raised chickens and turkeys. ("All Natural" on a poultry label is defined by the Department of

Agriculture as "minimally processed with no artificial ingredients." This claim on a whole bird only means that the bird has not been artificially basted, which is basically meaningless.) Shelton provides fresh poultry and other poultry–related products. Their chicken broth is excellent.

> Shelton Poultry
> 204 Loranne
> Pomona, CA 91767
> (909)623–4361

Sno–Pac provides a line of reasonably priced, organic frozen vegetables. Out with the old brands, loaded with chemicals, and in with Sno–Pac.

> Sno–Pac Foods Inc.
> 379 S. Pine Street
> Caledonia, MN 55921
> (507)724–5281

Spectrum Naturals' oils are expeller pressed without solvents. Both refined and unrefined oils are available. Their products range from oils and supplemental oils to cheese, mayonnaise, vinegars, dressings and sauces. Their brand names include Spectrum Naturals (oils), Veg–Omega, Sonnet Farms (cheese), Ayla's Organic (dressings) and Blue Banner.

> Spectrum Naturals, Inc.
> 133 Copeland Street
> Petaluma, CA 94952
> phone: (707)778–8900
> fax: (707)765–1026

Spring Tree Maple Syrup produces pure maple syrup. Pure maple syrup is far superior to the cheaper syrup mixes.

> Spring Tree Maple Syrup
> P.O. Box 1160
> Brattleboro, VT 05302
> phone: (802)254–8784
> fax: (802)254–8648

Sunspire is your answer to sugar–laden chocolate. Sunspire products contain no refined sugar and have a great taste. They can be purchased in carob, chocolate, mint and peanut. They provide confections and chocolate chips. They also have many dairy–free products.

> Sunspire
> 2114 Adams Avenue
> San Leandro, CA 94577
> (510)569–9731

VitaSpelt produces some of the best whole–grain pastas. They use whole–grain spelt, which many wheat–sensitive people can tolerate. Be sure to not overcook whole–grain pasta, as that will make it mushy. They have added a focacia bread, which can be used as an excellent pizza base. I have prepared many recipes for VitaSpelt products (with the brand name of Lifestyle for Health).

> VitaSpelt
> Purity Foods Inc.
> 2871 West Jolly Road
> Okemos, Ml 48864
> (800)99–SPELT

Westbrae and Little Bear are two excellent brands. The company is committed to organic and low–fat products. Little Bear, under the brand name Bearitos, has excellent chips, taco shells, tostada shells, popcorn, salsa, refried beans and pretzels. They also produce a licorice without refined sugar and additives. Westbrae has excellent snack food, cookies, soy milk, soy beverages and condiments.

Little Bear/Westbrae
1065 East Walnut Street
Carson, CA 90746
(310)886–8200

Bibliography

Baker, Elizabeth and Dr. Elton. *The UNcook Book.* Buena Vista, Colorado: Drelwood Publications, 1980.

Baker, Elizabeth and Dr. Elton. *Bandwagon to Health.* Saguache, Colorado: Drelwood Publications, 1984.

Barkie, Karen E. *Sweet & Sugarfree.* New York: St. Martin's Press, 1982.

Chiavetta, Janet B. *Eat, Drink And Be Healthy.* Raleigh, North Carolina: Piedmont Publishers, 1992.

Claiborne, Craig. *Craig Claiborne's The New New York Times Cookbook.* New York: Times Books, 1979.

Colbin, Annemarie. *The Book of Whole Meals.* New York: Ballantine Books, 1983.

Denver, Junior League of. *Creme de Colorado Cookbook.* Denver, Colorado: Junior League of Denver, 1987.

DuBelle, Lee. *Proper Food Combining Cookbook.* Phoenix, Arizona: Walsh and Associates, 1984.

Dunne, Lavon J. *Nutrition Almanac*, third edition. New York: McGraw Hill Publishing Company, 1990.

Ewalk, Ellen Buchman. *Recipes From a Small Planet.* New York: Ballantine Books, 1973.

Ford, Richard and Andersen, Joel. *Sea Green Primer.* Berkeley, California: Creative Arts Book Company, 1983.

Gerras, Charles. *Rodale's Basic Natural Foods Cookbook.* Emmaus, Pennsylvania: Rodale Press, 1984.

Hewitt, Jean. *The New York Times New Natural Foods Cookbook.* New York: Avon Books, 1982.

Jansen, Dr. Bernard. *Foods That Heal.* Garden City Park, New York: Avery Publishing Group, Inc., 1988.

Katzen, Mollie. *The Enchanted Broccoli Forest.* Berkeley, California: Ten Speed Press, 1982.

Katzen, Mollie. *Moosewood Cookbook.* Berkeley, California: Ten Speed Press, 1987.

Killeen, Jacqueline. *The Whole World Cookbook.* New York: Charles Scribner's Sons, 1979.

Lanigan, Anne. *The Yogurt Gourmet.* New York: Quick Fox, 1978.

Moosewood Collective. *New Recipes From Moosewood Restaurant.* Berkeley, California: Ten Speed Press, 1987.

Robertson, Laurel. *The New Laurel's Kitchen.* Berkeley, California: Ten Speed Press, 1986.

Shulman, Martha Rose. *Mediterranean LIGHT.* New York: Bantam Books, 1989.

Thomas, Anna. *The Vegetarian Epicure.* New York: Vintage Books, 1972.

Thomas, Anna. *The Vegetarian Epicure Book Two.* New York: Vintage Books, 1972.

Tribole, Evelyn, M.S., R.D. *Healthy Homestyle Cooking.* Emmaus, Pennsylvania: Rodale Press, 1994.

Whitaker, Donald R. and Flournoy, Barbara Durham. *Nature's Kitchen.* Lufkin Texas.

Wood, Rebecca. *Quinoa: The Supergrain.* New York: Kodansha, 1989.

Index

How can you make dinnertime easier?
. . . with your computer

and

Dinner!

Software to Help Busy People Make Great Meals in Minutes

Now there is a fun and practical software program--Dinner!--that helps you plan ahead and organize meals so that cooking them is easy. Dinner! gives you 16 weeks of seasonal menu plans. Simply select a weekly plan or create your own. Dinner! automatically gives you:

❖ A complete shopping list with everything you need at the store;

❖ Each recipe in your menu plan;

❖ A nutritional analysis and budget estimate; and

❖ Neat organized printouts to use in the kitchen and take to the store

Once you are organized like this, cooking meals is easy!

Turn the Page for More Information

more about. . .

Dinner!

- **Tasty, Lowfat Recipes and Menu Plans.** Dinner! comes with all the recipes from <u>Cookbook for the 90s</u>, a collection of tasty, lowfat recipes that are quick and easy, too.

- **Add-On Cookbooks on Disk**: Get more recipes and menu plans with these Cookbooks on Disk:

Lifestyle for Health $14.95
by Cheryl Townsley
Natural and whole foods collection with
180 recipes and 8 weekly menu plans.

Vegetarian Express: Easy Tasty, and Healthy Menus in 28 Minutes (or Less!) $15.95
By Nava Atlas and Lillian Kayte
Creative and quick vegetarian cooking with
150 recipes and 70 dinner menus.

- **Nutritional Information:** See the nutritional content of menu plans, recipes and ingredients.

- **Add and Organize Your Own Recipes:**   Nutritional content is calculated automatically

System Requirements

Windows:	Macintosh
386 IBM compatible PC or better	68020 processor or better
4 MB RAM	4 MB RAM
Windows 3.1 or higher	System 7 or higher
7 MB hard drive space	7 MB hard drive space

BOOKS –

Lifestyle for Health cookbook
by Cheryl Townsley

Delicious health food including: 8 weeks of menus and grocery lists, over 180 recipes with nutritional analysis, alternatives for sugar, white flour, fat, salt and dairy, many references, and more. **soft bound $20.00**
wire spiral bound $24.00

Meals in 30 Minutes
by Cheryl Townsley

Fast, easy, tasty meals in minutes. Includes menus, bulk cooking, freezer and leftover planning tips.   **$12.00**

Kids Favorites
by Cheryl Townsley

Information and recipes will help transition any person (birth to adult) from the average American diet to a healthier diet.   **$10.00**

Cookbook Special –

Set of All 3 Cookbooks – **$30.00**
(with wire bound LFH – **$35.00**)

FoodSmart!
by Cheryl Townsley

Cheryl shares her compelling story from suicide attempt and near death to health. Learn how to become emotionally and mentally healthy, as well as physically healthy. A great story that provides practical insight, along with many practical helps.   **$12.00**

Vegetarian Dining Using Tofu & Tempeh
by Cheryl Townsley

Delicious recipes with low fat, sugar–free and dairy–free options.   Booklet   **$ 6.50**

Gift Baskets
by Cheryl Townsley

Learn how to make beautiful gift baskets from grocery sacks and fill with healthy, easy–to–make gifts.   Booklet   **$6.50**

Cookie Exchange
by Cheryl Townsley

Over 30 quick cookies with low fat, sugar–free and dairy–free options.   Booklet   **$6.50**

NEWSLETTER –

Lifestyle for Health

10 pages of nutritional information, recipes, health updates, new products and a touch of humor.   6 issues/year – **$16.00**

SOFTWARE –

Dinner! and Lifestyle for Health cookbook on disk

This computer software is easy to use, effective and a real time saver!

Includes 16 weeks of seasonal menus, recipes, grocery lists and nutritional charts — PLUS the capability to add and analyze your own recipes.

Available for IBM & Macintosh computers. System requirements — 386 or higher IBM compatible PC • 4MB RAM • Microsoft Windows 3.1 or higher • 7.5 MB hard drive space

Add $4.00 shipping/handling per item to order instead of 15‰.
Please specify MAC or IBM PC on order form.   **$65.00**

SUPPLEMENTS –

3–D Cleanser

Helps to cleanse the colon, kidneys, liver and blood. 32 oz. bottle, one month supply.   **$18.95**

Multi–Vitamin and Mineral Formula

Provides 100–200‰ of the RDA of 16 vitamins and minerals. 60 tablets/bottle, two months supply.   **$18.95**

Vegetable & Fruit Concentrate

Provides the daily equivalent of five servings of vegetables and fruit. Contains live food enzymes needed to release the energy stored in vitamins and nutrients. 120 tablets/bottle, one month supply.   **$17.95**

All prices subject to change.

ORDER FORM

ITEM NAME	QTY.	PRICE	TOTAL
	Subtotal		
	Shipping & Handling — add 15%		
	Tax (CO residents add 3.8%)		
	Total Enclosed		

Name _____

Address _____

City _____ State _____ Zip _____

Day Phone (___) _____

Send check or money order to:
Lifestyle for Health • P.O. Box 3871 • Littleton, CO 80161 • (303) 771-9357